FACULTY-LIBRARIAN COLLABORATIONS:

Integrating the Information Literacy Framework into Disciplinary Courses

edited by

Michael Stöpel, Livia Piotto, Xan Goodman, and Samantha Godbey

Association of College and Research Libraries
A division of the American Library Association
Chicago, Illinois 2020

The paper used in this publication meets the minimum requirements of American National Standard for Information Sciences–Permanence of Paper for Printed Library Materials, ANSI Z39.48-1992. ∞

Library of Congress Control Number: 2020950678

Printed in the United States of America.

24 23 22 21 20 5 4 3 2 1

Table of Contents

Preface

I am not sure where to start the story of the workshop that launched this collection. Maybe it started when I attended the ACRL Immersion Program in 2014 and asked myself why the disciplinary faculty didn't attend these workshops. Maybe it started during the AMICAL focus group discussions on information literacy in 2015, when I spoke to one of the AMICAL librarians, who said that she never meets with faculty. Or maybe it started when I began teaching information literacy at American University of Paris (AUP) in 2010 and considered where librarians could intervene and co-teach in our first-year experience program.

When we, the AMICAL Information Literacy Committee, looked into organizing an information literacy workshop for our fellow librarians and for ourselves, ACRL was about to publish the at-the-time new ACRL *Framework for Information Literacy for Higher Education*.[1] We had heard Lori Townsend during the 2015 AMICAL Conference speaking about threshold concepts,[2] which had encouraged us to integrate these new concepts into instruction and the curriculum in general. We were also impressed by the workshop presented by Samantha Godbey and Xan Goodman on thresholds and redesigning lesson plans during the 2015 European Conference on Information Literacy (ECIL),[3] which we were able to attend thanks to an AMICAL grant.

So the ball was in our court to set up a meaningful workshop taking those elements into account. "Co-design: Integrating Information Literacy into Your Disciplinary Course" was the result.[4] Two signature elements of the workshop were the faculty-librarian collaboration and the work to integrate the ACRL Framework into a disciplinary course. Inspired by the ACRL tradition of hands-on learning, we applied the ACRL Immersion philosophy to the AMICAL context, asking potential participants to send an application to us including a concrete project they would like to co-design (and teach) for the following semester (fall 2017). Potential participants were asked to apply in teams, as we believed that a meaningful course integration would work only when both instructors—faculty and librarian—would be sitting at the same table. Of course, this was not innocent: the workshop also aimed to work with and promote the

ACRL Framework concepts because they were new to most participants and—as we believe—of value to all participants.

The benefit of the application process and the project-driven approach was to give potential participants time to think ahead about what they would like to work on during the workshop. As an intentional side effect, the application process also required participants to agree in advance to work together on a project they had chosen together. This served as an icebreaking activity that initiated the collaboration between the two instructors even before the workshop had started.[5]

A final important element of the workshop was that we asked potential participants to commit to an assessment effort at the end of their teaching experience in fall 2017 so that we could explore the impact of the co-design workshop on teaching and learning. AMICAL director Jeff Gima had suggested adding this element to the workshop in order to provide feedback to the Mellon Foundation, which is the main funding source for the AMICAL Consortium. We therefore conducted a survey of participants in spring 2018 to gather feedback and initial stories of the various co-design adventures. These stories served as a starting point for the collection of case studies and lesson plans that my co-editors and I share here.

Rendre à César ce qui est à César

Before letting you, dear reader, go off and read, I would like to thank everybody who was involved in this project, as projects like this are not built in one day and are built only with the help of many. Thank you to the AMICAL Information Literacy Committee members at the time of the workshop—Chris, Tatev, Livia, Madeline, and Krassi for inspiration and enthusiasm; Samantha and Xan, our fantastic workshop leaders; Jeff Gima, the AMICAL director, for fruitful conversations, feedback, and support for the project; the whole AUP library team—Jorge the library director, Isabelle, Iulia, Monica, and Lily—who served as hands on deck when needed to provide a warm welcome and setup of food and facilities; Brenda and Sinead from Academic Affairs for choosing the right *traiteur* and *hôtels* in the neighborhood; the maintenance team for the room setup and being there on time to open and close the building; Phil for security; ITS for the wireless; Mathieu for the multimedia setup; the twenty-eight workshop participants for their good mood; Erin and Judith from ACRL for the valuable feedback and time to bring this book to life; and, last but not least, Celeste Schenck, AUP president and one of the founding members of AMICAL, for her wonderful opening remarks that set the tone and spirit of the workshop.

With best regards and greetings to our fellows at AMICAL and beyond.

Bonne lecture!

Michael Stöpel
User Services Librarian, American University of Paris
Chair, AMICAL Information Literacy Committee

Notes

1. Association of College and Research Libraries, *Framework for Information Literacy for Higher Education* (Chicago: Association of College and Research Libraries, 2016).
2. Lori Townsend, "Negotiating Thresholds: Conflict and Transformation in the Liminal Space" (presentation, AMICAL 2015 Conference, American University in Bulgaria, Blagoevgrad, Bulgaria, May 29, 2015), https://www.amicalnet.org/sessions/negotiating-thresholds.
3. Samantha Godbey, Xan Goodman, and Susan Wainscott, "Crossing the Threshold with Threshold Concepts: Redesigning a Library Instruction Lesson Plan" (workshop, European Conference on Information Literacy [ECIL], Tallinn, Estonia, October 19, 2015).
4. Samantha Godbey and Xan Goodman, "Co-design: Integrating Information Literacy into Your Disciplinary Course" (AMICAL workshop, American University of Paris, March 31–April 1, 2017), https://www.amicalnet.org/events/co-design-integrating-information-literacy-into-your-disciplinary-course.
5. I use the term *instructors* intentionally in this context as I want to move beyond the common distinction between faculty and librarians. Librarians are deeply engaged in instruction, and faculty do recognize this.

Bibliography

Association of College and Research Libraries. *Framework for Information Literacy for Higher Education*. Chicago: Association of College and Research Libraries, 2016.

Godbey, Samantha, and Xan Goodman. "Co-design: Integrating Information Literacy into Your Disciplinary Course." AMICAL workshop, American University of Paris, March 31–April 1, 2017. https://www.amicalnet.org/events/co-design-integrating-information-literacy-into-your-disciplinary-course.

Godbey, Samantha, Xan Goodman, and Susan Wainscott. "Crossing the Threshold with Threshold Concepts: Redesigning a Library Instruction Lesson Plan." Workshop, European Conference on Information Literacy (ECIL), Tallinn, Estonia, October 19, 2015.

Townsend, Lori. "Negotiating Thresholds: Conflict and Transformation in the Liminal Space." Presentation, AMICAL 2015 Conference, American University in Bulgaria, Blagoevgrad, Bulgaria, May 29, 2015. https://www.amicalnet.org/sessions/negotiating-thresholds.

Introduction

Livia Piotto*

Reference and Instruction Coordinator, Frohring Library, John Cabot University, Rome, Italy

Christine Furno*

Reference and Instruction Librarian, American University of Sharjah, United Arab Emirates

This book is a collection of case studies and lesson plans that arose out of work done in the workshop "Co-design: Integrating Information Literacy into Your Disciplinary Course," sponsored by the AMICAL Consortium in spring 2017.[1]

AMICAL Overview

The AMICAL Consortium, founded in 2004 at the American University of Paris, at present brings together twenty-nine higher education institutions located in twenty-two countries across Eastern, Central and Western Europe; West and North Africa; the Middle East; and Central and Southern Asia. Most of the participating institutions are autonomous entities accredited by American agencies and are not affiliated with US-based institutions. Full and affiliate members of the consortium commit to supporting the liberal arts curriculum and are also members of the Association of American International Colleges and Universities (AAICU).

The mission of the AMICAL Consortium is "to advance learning, teaching and research through the collaborative development of library and information services and curricular resources at member institutions."[2] The development of the consortium activities throughout the years has been made possible thanks to the support of the Andrew W. Mellon Foundation, together with annual contributions from AMICAL's member institutions.

---

* Authors are AMICAL Information Literacy Committee Members

All AMICAL institutions work in their national and local contexts, each one of them with its own peculiar political, legal, economic, cultural, and social considerations. Despite their individuality, each institution is characterized by an intrinsic American essence as an American-style institution located outside the United States. The support of AMICAL in terms of alignment to American standards and professional development opportunities is essential in helping member institutions connect to similar institutions and avoid being too isolated.

AMICAL organizes an annual conference that, throughout the years, has become an important opportunity for its members to meet face-to-face, discuss shared issues, and strengthen collaborative ties. There is a strong influence of librarians in the consortium because it was initially created by libraries. In subsequent years, however, the consortium expanded its scope and audience to incorporate faculty-librarian collaboration. At the AMICAL Conference in 2013, for example, the consortium introduced themes of new literacies and emphasized library-IT-faculty collaboration.

The annual conference is also the moment during which the standing committees, created to support and spread the consortium's work among participating institutions, have the opportunity to reconnect and share accomplishments from the previous year. The consortium mission is advanced by all committees, including the Information Literacy Committee, whose mandate is to promote the essential role of information literacy within the liberal arts curriculum and to support a culture of collaboration between the library and the faculty to incorporate a critical pedagogy perspective.

Information Literacy at AMICAL Institutions

Although the Information Literacy Committee attempts to track best practices for instruction throughout the consortium, a true systematic review of the library instruction programs across AMICAL was done as part of a broader research project about American-style libraries outside the United States.[3]

Previous information literacy research conducted by the Information Literacy Committee included focus groups administered at the 2015 AMICAL Conference. The session, "Information Literacy Perspectives—Focus Groups with Faculty and Librarians," set out to investigate if and how information literacy is integrated into the curriculum across the various AMICAL institutions.[4] Results were presented at the 2015 European Conference on Information Literacy (ECIL) held in Tallinn, Estonia.[5] The focus groups aimed to describe how information literacy was taught and at what level it was integrated into the curriculum of the various AMICAL institutions; perspectives of both librarians and faculty members were analyzed, which brought to light a certain disconnect in terms of understanding basic information literacy concepts. On the other hand, the focus groups also highlighted the importance of collaboration and support between faculty and librarians to reach full integration of information literacy instruction into the curriculum.

The focus group results were the initial spark that gave the Information Literacy Committee the idea for a workshop that would have faculty and librarians working together to integrate the ACRL *Framework for Information Literacy for Higher Education* into a course.[6] Most AMICAL instruction librarians come from a non-US, multicultural education background, while their day-to-day work is grounded in American educational standards. However, they do not have easy access to professional development activities in the field. Therefore, the Information Literacy Committee felt that the adoption of the new ACRL Framework was an important opportunity to provide practical professional development aligned with recent developments in information literacy instruction. Among its activities, the Information Literacy Committee strives to create opportunities for consortium members to maintain high quality standards in their library instruction programs, and the workshop "Co-design: Integrating Information Literacy into Your Disciplinary Course," held at the American University of Paris in spring 2017, was one of them.[7] Participants worked together for two days to plan how they would integrate the ACRL Framework into a pilot course in fall 2017.

The workshop was a big success in terms of interest, although not all AMICAL institutions could participate due to the financial and logistical constraints of a professional development opportunity such as the co-design workshop. A large part of the success of the workshop itself was the fact that the AMICAL librarians are already a strong community, and the participants were already familiar with each other and with the peculiarities of each individual institution. The workshop leaders were pleasantly surprised by this situation, which laid the groundwork for the collaborative environment of the workshop itself.

This Collection

Faculty-Librarian Collaborations: Integrating the Information Literacy Framework into Disciplinary Courses is a product of what the workshop participants accomplished after the Paris workshop. In the chapter "Designing a Collaborative Learning Experience around the Framework," Xan Goodman and Samantha Godbey, the two workshop leaders, describe how the workshop was designed and developed. "Insights into Faculty-Librarian Collaborations around the Framework: Findings from the 2018 Co-design Survey," the chapter written by AMICAL's Information Literacy Committee members, discusses the results of the survey administered to workshop participants at the end of the pilot courses. The results are analyzed in depth, and recommendations and future implications are drawn.

The bulk of the content in this collection consists of case studies and lesson plans. These case studies represent a selection of the collaborations developed out of the workshop. A selection of information literacy lesson plans based on the ACRL Framework and co-designed by librarians and faculty are also included. Some lesson plans come directly from the pilot courses, and others have been inspired by the principles outlined during the workshop.

As you read the various case studies and lesson plans, we hope you will be inspired to modify and apply a study or plan that resonates with your individual instructional context—wherever in the world that may be.

Notes

1. Samantha Godbey and Xan Goodman, "Co-design: Integrating Information Literacy into Your Disciplinary Course" (AMICAL workshop, American University of Paris, March 31–April 1, 2017), https://www.amicalnet.org/events/co-design-integrating-information-literacy-into-your-disciplinary-course.
2. "About: The Mission and History of the AMICAL Consortium," AMICAL Consortium, https://www.amicalnet.org/about.
3. Amanda B. Click and Meggan Houlihan, "Library Instruction Programs at American-Style Academic Libraries outside of the United States," in *Bridging Worlds: Emerging Models and Practices of U.S. Academic Libraries around the Globe*, ed. Raymond Pun, Scott Collard, and Justin Parrott (Chicago: Association of College and Research Libraries, 2016), 139–60.
4. AMICAL Information Literacy Committee, "Information Literacy Perspectives—Focus Groups with Faculty and Librarians" (focus groups session, AMICAL 2015 Conference, American University in Bulgaria, Blagoevgrad, Bulgaria, May 27–30, 2015).

5. Christine Furno et al., "Do All Roads Lead to Rome? Have We Integrated Information Literacy into the Curriculum?" (poster presentation, Third European Conference on Information Literacy [ECIL], Tallinn, Estonia, October 19–22, 2015).
6. Association of College and Research Libraries, *Framework for Information Literacy for Higher Education* (Chicago: Association of College and Research Libraries, 2016).
7. Godbey and Goodman, "Co-design."

Bibliography

AMICAL Consortium. "About: The Mission and History of the AMICAL Consortium." https://www.amicalnet.org/about.

AMICAL Information Literacy Committee. "Information Literacy Perspectives—Focus Groups with Faculty and Librarians." Focus groups session, AMICAL 2015 Conference, American University in Bulgaria, Blagoevgrad, Bulgaria, May 27–30, 2015.

Association of College and Research Libraries. *Framework for Information Literacy for Higher Education*. Chicago: Association of College and Research Libraries, 2016.

Click, Amanda B., and Meggan Houlihan. "Library Instruction Programs at American-Style Academic Libraries outside of the United States." In *Bridging Worlds: Emerging Models and Practices of U.S. Academic Libraries around the Globe*. Edited by Raymond Pun, Scott Collard, and Justin Parrott, 139–60. Chicago: Association of College and Research Libraries, 2016.

Furno, Christine, Madeline Mundt, Livia Piotto, Michael Stöpel, and Tatevik Zargaryan. "Do All Roads Lead to Rome? Have We Integrated Information Literacy into the Curriculum?" Poster presentation, Third European Conference on Information Literacy (ECIL), Tallinn, Estonia, October 19–22, 2015.

Godbey, Samantha, and Xan Goodman. "Co-design: Integrating Information Literacy into Your Disciplinary Course." AMICAL workshop, American University of Paris, March 31–April 1, 2017. https://www.amicalnet.org/events/co-design-integrating-information-literacy-into-your-disciplinary-course.

SECTION I
Chapters

CHAPTER 1

Designing a Collaborative Learning Experience around the Framework

Xan Goodman

Health Sciences Librarian, Associate Professor, University of Nevada, Las Vegas, USA

Samantha Godbey

Education Librarian, Associate Professor, University of Nevada, Las Vegas, USA

In late 2015, we presented a three-hour workshop on the nascent ACRL *Framework for Information Literacy for Higher Education* at the European Conference on Information Literacy (ECIL) in Tallinn, Estonia,[1] after which we were approached about preparing a more in-depth learning experience on the Framework for a group of international librarians. These librarians were part of the AMICAL Consortium, a consortium of twenty-nine liberal arts institutions in Europe, Asia, and Africa. At this point, we had already led several active learning–filled workshops on the Framework, including the one at ECIL. We were also working on a coedited book on the Framework, which would eventually be published as *Disciplinary Applications of Information Literacy Threshold Concepts.*[2] Through these projects, we had met librarians from across the United States and throughout the world who were eager to engage more deeply with the Framework and the concepts it contains. Although other information literacy standards and guidelines exist and are used widely in international contexts, we had direct experience with international librarians who, like their American counterparts, were struggling with how to transition into working with the Framework.

Although there are, of course, benefits to discussing information literacy among librarians, the successful integration of information literacy into the curriculum requires collaboration between librarians and disciplinary faculty. Therefore, we felt that it would be ideal to bring both together to engage around this new approach to information literacy. We worked with the chair of the AMICAL Information Literacy Committee to develop a proposal to the AMICAL organization, and it was selected as a professional development offering in spring 2017. Titled "Co-design: Integrating Information Literacy into Your Disciplinary Course," this two-day, hands-on learning experience was open to librarians and disciplinary faculty partners from AMICAL member institutions.[3] The workshop was designed to provide an opportunity for faculty and librarians to work together on advancing information literacy at their institutions by engaging directly with the new Framework. In this chapter, we describe the workshop itself, which laid the groundwork for the collaborations detailed in the case studies and lesson plans in this collection.

Fourteen pairs participated in the workshop. In addition to four teams from the host institution, American University of Paris (AUP), other participants traveled from Armenia, Bulgaria, Italy, Kosovo, Kuwait, Kyrgyzstan, Lebanon, Morocco, Switzerland, and the United Arab Emirates to work on courses such as history, writing, media studies, political science, marketing, and cultural anthropology. Courses ranged from first-year seminars to graduate-level courses. Six of these teams received funding for airfare and housing, while others were self-funded, which speaks to the deep interest and commitment to this project. Each pair provided in their application clear plans for close collaboration on the planning and teaching of a course for the following semester; these plans were solidified in the workshop itself.

Workshop Design

We designed the workshop using a backward design approach, starting with developing learning outcomes and working backward through the assessments and activities that would enable our participants to scaffold student learning and measure progress toward the desired outcomes. Additionally, we wanted to incorporate active learning throughout, reducing time spent lecturing and emphasizing activities that called for the active participation of the workshop participants.

We wanted to ensure that participants had tangible products that they could take back to their institutions. Participants would finish the workshop with a draft of a codeveloped syllabus, including collaboratively identified learning outcomes and ideas for assignments, lesson plans, and assessment strategies. Participants would also articulate an implementation plan for the collaboration itself. As part of the requirements for participation from the sponsoring organization, participants would put these syllabi and implementation plans into practice in a pilot course in fall 2017 and would report back in spring 2018 on lessons learned after implementing the pilot course.

The Workshop

First, we required prework of all participants. Participants were asked to read two documents: the Framework itself, including the introduction, and an article or chapter selected by the disciplinary faculty member about core concepts in their discipline. Selections by disciplinary faculty included chapters from textbooks providing overviews of their disciplines, as well as articles or chapters that explored a concept that would be a focus of the course, such as diversity and literature or critical media literacy.[4]

The workshop itself was structured around the backward design model, starting with developing outcomes. Further, we modeled throughout the kinds of active learning strategies and assessment techniques that participants might consider incorporating into the plans they were developing themselves, such as brainstorming, Think-Pair-Share, jigsaws, and one-minute papers. During the two days of the workshop, participants were reading, discussing, questioning, and often moving around the room. They were composing, rethinking, and revising. As facilitators, we designed a structured workshop plan that allowed for flexibility to accommodate changes that might be necessary along the way. The first day was more structured, while the second day provided more opportunities for participants to work with their partner on course and assignment design.

The workshop space was arranged in groups of tables with four to six participants at each table group. In addition to the participants, two additional AUP library staff observed the workshop and assisted with logistics such as registration and coffee breaks.

Day 1

9:00–9:15	Welcome
9:15–10:30	Session 1: Introductions, Materials, Workshop Plan
10:30–10:45	Coffee Break
10:45–12:00	Session 2: Information Literacy and the Framework
12:00–13:30	Lunch
13:30–15:00	Session 3: Applying the Framework to Courses (+ Draft/ Revise Course Learning Outcomes)
15:00–15:15	Coffee Break
15:15–16:45	Session 4: Applying the Framework—Draft Lesson Plan, Framework Resources

In the morning of the first day, we focused on getting to know each other and the Framework. The librarians in the workshop already knew each other from the library consortium, but we felt it was important for the disciplinary faculty to be incorporated into the learning community and for all participants to have at least a preliminary understanding of each other's projects. We started with a twenty-minute icebreaker that asked participants to reflect on, and then discuss, a course or assignment that had changed their way of thinking. Then we went through introductions of all participants, including their institution, role, discipline or specialty, and a brief description of the course they were focusing on.

The next segment of the workshop explored changing definitions of information literacy. We did a brief lecture defining information literacy and providing an overview of the Framework; then participants discussed the question "What does information literacy mean or look like in your discipline?" This was an opportunity for participants to discuss personal experiences with information literacy as well as drawing on the shared readings that had been the prework for the workshop.

From this broad discussion of information literacy, we moved into more specific discussions of the content of the Framework. We delivered a brief lecture about the individual frames, but the detailed work of exploring the frames was done by the participants. Each table group was assigned a frame to discuss in detail ("How would you explain this frame? What resonates for you and your students?") before returning to the whole group for a frame-by-frame discussion of the Framework. We anticipated from previous workshop experience that this segment would likely require a substantial chunk of time, particularly for participants who were new to the Framework, and this activity continued after lunch.

In the afternoon, we started the work of applying the Framework to the courses. Drawing on Middendorf and Pace's Decoding the Disciplines model,[5] we encouraged pairs to identify potential bottlenecks in student learning in their courses. We first did an activity in which we provided scenarios for discussion.[6] For each scenario, participants were asked to identify a potential bottleneck and to identify a frame from the Framework that might help alleviate this bottleneck. This discussion provided participants with tangible examples of how the concepts in the Framework might be used to rethink the student learning experience.

Participants then worked with their partners to articulate bottlenecks in the specific course they had come to work on, draft course outcomes, and identify a frame or frames that aligned with these outcomes. These outcomes could be cognitive or affective and might incorporate language from the Framework itself as was helpful. The draft outcomes were shared on big paper and posted on the walls so that participants could read and comment on each other's outcomes before proceeding.

In the final segments of the day, participants identified a priority point in the course for a single librarian session. Participants wrote a draft lesson plan, with the understanding that these were initial thoughts on how to use the librarian and a reminder that the materials would all be revised the following day as we moved into discussing assessment and learning activities. Participants were reminded to try to make connections between the bottlenecks they had identified, their course outcomes, and the Framework. We provided focused work time to explore the Framework and related online resources or to work on syllabi or course outcomes.

This marked the end of the first day, in which we had begun thinking deeply about the Framework and laid the foundation for the faculty-librarian collaboration now underway.

Day 2

9:00–9:15	Welcome + Review
9:15–10:30	Session 1: Assessment
10:30–10:45	Coffee Break
10:45–12:00	Session 2: Learning Activities

12:00–13:30	Lunch
13:30–15:00	Session 3: Group Peer Review
15:00–15:15	Coffee Break
15:15–16:45	Session 4: Implementation Plan + Workshop Evaluation

On the second day of the workshop, our goal was to have draft plans, including draft syllabi, course outcomes, and assessments, in place by the lunch break. Having articulated student bottlenecks, course outcomes, and connections to the Framework on the first day, we continued the backward design process to work on assessment. Some participants were hesitant about assessment, having experienced assessment primarily as an administrative requirement in the past. Many felt anxious about doing assessment correctly or about how the data they gathered might be used. This was true for both librarians and disciplinary faculty. In the workshop, we acknowledged and discussed these worries, but we encouraged participants to draw their focus back to the student experience. We defined assessment as evidence of student learning or experience: that is, how will the instructors know what students have learned or experienced as related to their course outcomes? We also discussed approaches to responding to student work and coding assessment data.

We started with a brief lecture on types of assessment and an activity to help participants expand their ideas about assessment. From our experience, we knew that faculty frequently use research papers to assess student learning. Therefore, we provided a list of alternative assessments to open up other ways of thinking about assessment, including several examples of alternatives to a research paper such as writing a grant proposal, preparing a marketing plan, or creating an infographic. Participants read, annotated, and commented on a list of potential assessments, noting ones they had tried, what they might want to try, and which ones were unclear. After participants annotated and commented on this list of assessments individually, we discussed the list as a group. At this point, we answered many questions about unfamiliar assessments and discussed possible variations on these assessments that might work for their courses.

Participants then worked with their partners to identify at least one assessment for each course outcome. Participants were encouraged to identify student-focused, authentic assessments for the overall course as well as any specific sessions they had in mind for the semester.

Continuing to work backward from their course outcomes, we next devoted time to discuss specific learning activities that could be used to help students be successful on the assessments. We worked our way through the same annotate-and-discuss activity we had used for assessment. In this case, we provided a two-page list of instruction activities. This list included a range of student-centered, active learning approaches, such as concept mapping, fishbowl discussions, jigsaws, and Think-Pair-Share. Additionally, throughout the workshop, we had explicitly noted learning strategies used in the workshop, identifying each active learning strategy by name in the instructions for each task we did together. Participants again read, annotated, and commented on the list provided, noting learning activities they had already tried, what they'd like to try, and which were unclear. After this individual time to process, we discussed the learning and instruction activities as a whole group.

Next, we provided participants thirty minutes of focused work time to pull their materials together. Each pair needed to finalize their course outcomes and assessments. They also completed a semester timeline handout to plan out how the different assessments and activities would fit together over time. It is important to note that for each of these tasks, participants were encouraged to revise earlier products as needed, checking each for connections to the Framework and reworking components in an iterative process.

Regarding the structure of the work materials, we provided handouts for each of the following: lesson plan template, assessment, and a semester timeline. Each pair was encouraged to use these as loosely or strictly as was helpful to them. Some pairs found the structure of the handouts to be helpful and completed all handouts very carefully, choosing to revise their official syllabus after the workshop was complete. Others found it more useful to use the handouts to jot down some ideas and questions but primarily worked on revising their syllabus directly.

The next portion of the workshop was devoted to group peer review of materials. For the group peer review, we provided the following questions and criteria to guide participant feedback. Each pair met with at least two other pairs for twenty minutes each.

For course outcomes, we encouraged participants to consider these questions:

- Are course outcomes clear?
- Are they appropriate for these learners?
- Do they relate to a frame or frames from the Framework?
- Are students given multiple opportunities to engage with these ideas?

For the assignments and assessments, we asked participants to consider the extent to which the assignments:

- align with the course goals
- are relevant or authentic (replicate real-world tasks, realistic)
- provide opportunities for students to receive feedback
- are combined with appropriate learning activities that prepare students for success in larger assignments

During the final session of the day, participants planned ahead for continuing the collaboration beyond this workshop. We provided an open-ended implementation plan handout to prompt this planning. This included questions such as:

- What do you need to do next in order to successfully implement this plan?
- How will the group maintain communication?
- How often should the group meet?
- What information should be shared among group members, and who is responsible for dissemination?
- What will you do with the assessment data? When?

Then it was time to close the workshop. We revisited the definition of information literacy from the Framework, which we had discussed on the morning of the first day. At this point, we wanted to discuss in what ways participants' understanding of information literacy and how it applies to their discipline had changed over the course of our work together. Participants shared successes and frustrations from their work through this process. For many of the disciplinary faculty, information literacy was a new concept. For many of the librarians, rethinking information literacy as a "set of integrated abilities"[7] required a shift in thinking. For all, having two days of time devoted to discussing these ideas was invaluable to even begin the process of integrating information literacy into the curriculum.

Thinking Ahead

In the next chapter, our AMICAL colleagues discuss the results of the survey completed by participants. As facilitators, we integrated assessment into the workshop plan so that we could respond to participant needs during the workshop, and we collected evaluations at the end of day two.

It is important to note that some participants struggled with the idea of threshold concepts and the other theories discussed in the Framework. Some participants needed more time to digest the terminology from the Framework than we were able to provide. We provided an introduction to the main theories discussed in the Framework document, including threshold concepts, but we tried to do so quickly in order to devote more time to the frames themselves. We had at least one professor who needed much more time to grapple with these new ideas. This participant wanted time to read extensively about these ideas before proceeding to examine the specific content of the frames. As a scholar, this professor felt it was important to internalize and trust the theories mentioned in the Framework before engaging with it fully. Drawing on threshold concept terminology, some participants were working through a liminal space and experiencing the frustration that often comes with making changes to one's thinking. Although we tried to flip some learning by requiring reading before the workshop, we witnessed firsthand this bottleneck in learning during the workshop sessions.

If we were to run another workshop, we would be sure to highlight these theories in advance in order to allow time for participants to work through the liminal space. The theory component seemed to be especially challenging for disciplinary faculty, either because of their academic training in specific theories or because information literacy was new to them. Increasing prework resources and explaining this potential bottleneck in advance could help to alleviate this challenge. This challenge was also exacerbated by the condensed nature of this workshop. Liminality is real, and adjusting to entirely new concepts cannot necessarily take place on schedule within a two-day learning experience.

Additionally, participants expressed a strong desire for time with the workshop facilitators for one-on-one meetings to discuss their projects. We made an effort to circulate among participants throughout the workshop and provide feedback along the way, and we structured the workshop so that each pair would receive feedback from four to six other participants and view at least two other final projects. However, we did not meet with each of the fourteen pairs individually. Given the overwhelming interest expressed by the participants, we discussed how we might schedule these appointment slots during lunch or coffee breaks. While this places a strain on the facilitators, we felt that this should be a priority in the future. Ideally, we would extend the workshop by an additional half day to accommodate these appointments.

While there are, of course, aspects we would modify for the future, overall we are proud of the work done here. The co-design workshop was a productive, laughter-filled two days of exploring new ideas and thinking deeply about what is important to our students. We are grateful for the experience of working with these thoughtful, engaged librarians and professors. We hope that the chapters in this collection are helpful to you, the reader, as you consider how the Framework might be useful in your own work. We hope that you are able to find ways of collaborating with colleagues across your campus to integrate information literacy into the curriculum, ways that are meaningful to you and the students we serve.

Notes

1. Association of College and Research Libraries, *Framework for Information Literacy for Higher Education* (Chicago: Association of College and Research Libraries, 2016); Samantha Godbey, Xan Goodman, and Susan Wainscott, "Crossing the Threshold with Threshold Concepts: Redesigning a Library Instruction Lesson Plan" (workshop, European Conference on Information Literacy [ECIL], Tallinn, Estonia, October 19, 2015).
2. Samantha Godbey, Susan Wainscott, and Xan Goodman, eds., *Disciplinary Applications of Information Literacy Threshold Concepts* (Chicago: Association of College and Research Libraries, 2017).
3. Samantha Godbey and Xan Goodman, "Co-design: Integrating Information Literacy into Your Disciplinary Course" (AMICAL workshop, American University of Paris, March 31–April 1, 2017), https://www.amicalnet.org/events/co-design-integrating-information-literacy-into-your-disciplinary-course.
4. Masao Miyoshi, "Turn to the Planet: Literature, Diversity, and Totality," *Comparative Literature* 53, no. 4 (2001): 283–97; Steven Funk, Douglas Kellner, and Jeff Share, "Critical Media Literacy as Transformative Pedagogy," in *Handbook of Research on Media Literacy in the Digital Age*, ed. Melda N. Yildiz and Jared Keengwe (Hershey, PA: IGI Global, 2016), 1–30.
5. Joan Middendorf and David Pace, "Decoding the Disciplines: A Model for Helping Students Learn Disciplinary Ways of Thinking," *New Directions for Teaching and Learning* 2004, no. 98 (Summer 2004): 1–12, https://doi.org/10.1002/tl.142.
6. The examples for these scenarios were drawn from our coedited book Godbey, Wainscott, and Goodman, *Disciplinary Applications*.
7. Association of College and Research Libraries, *Framework*.

Bibliography

Association of College and Research Libraries. *Framework for Information Literacy for Higher Education*. Chicago: Association of College and Research Libraries, 2016.

Funk, Steven, Douglas Kellner, and Jeff Share. "Critical Media Literacy as Transformative Pedagogy." In *Handbook of Research on Media Literacy in the Digital Age*. Edited by Melda N. Yildiz and Jared Keengwe, 1–30. Hershey, PA: IGI Global, 2016.

Godbey, Samantha, and Xan Goodman. "Co-design: Integrating Information Literacy into Your Disciplinary Course." AMICAL workshop, American University of Paris, March 31–April 1, 2017. https://www.amicalnet.org/events/co-design-integrating-information-literacy-into-your-disciplinary-course.

Godbey, Samantha, Xan Goodman, and Susan Wainscott. "Crossing the Threshold with Threshold Concepts: Redesigning a Library Instruction Lesson Plan." Workshop, European Conference on Information Literacy (ECIL), Tallinn, Estonia, October 19, 2015.

Godbey, Samantha, Susan Wainscott, and Xan Goodman, eds. *Disciplinary Applications of Information Literacy Threshold Concepts*. Chicago: Association of College and Research Libraries, 2017.

Middendorf, Joan, and David Pace. "Decoding the Disciplines: A Model for Helping Students Learn Disciplinary Ways of Thinking." *New Directions for Teaching and Learning* 2004, no. 98 (Summer 2004): 1–12. https://doi.org/10.1002/tl.142.

Miyoshi, Masao. "Turn to the Planet: Literature, Diversity, and Totality." *Comparative Literature* 53, no. 4 (2001): 283–97.

CHAPTER 2

Insights into Faculty-Librarian Collaborations around the Framework

Findings from the 2018 Co-design Survey

Michael Stöpel*

User Services Librarian, American University of Paris, France

Livia Piotto*

Reference and Instruction Coordinator, Frohring Library, John Cabot University, Rome, Italy

Christine Furno*

Reference and Instruction Librarian, American University of Sharjah, United Arab Emirates

Krasimir Spasov*

Information Literacy Librarian, American University in Bulgaria

Tatev Zargaryan*

Library Systems and E-services Librarian, American University of Armenia

* Authors are AMICAL Information Literacy Committee Members

Introduction

Since the 1980s, assessment has been one of the most frequently investigated topics in library and information science literature,[1] seen by librarians as a valid tool for analyzing the effectiveness and impact of teaching. With this in mind, after the Paris workshop and the rollout of the co-designed pilot courses,[2] the AMICAL Information Literacy Committee (ILC) wanted to assess whether the courses had been successful with regard to both learning and teaching and to determine new fruits the co-designing had produced. A second, but equally important, motivation was to report back to the AMICAL Consortium, which funded and supported our project from the beginning. The main goal was to collect qualitative feedback to give insight into the projects and to build a "thick description" of the teaching experience.[3] In order to effectively assess the course design project, as well as provide essential feedback to our stakeholders, the ILC developed and administered a survey about the co-design experience.

This survey was conducted among twenty-six participants from eleven different liberal arts institutions outside the United States that are all members of the AMICAL Consortium (appendix 2A). The survey participants came from diverse countries: Lebanon, Armenia, the United Arab Emirates, Morocco, Kuwait, Italy, Switzerland, Kyrgyzstan, Bulgaria, Kosovo, and France. It is interesting to see how the teaching experience and the idea of liberal arts education unfolds within the local contexts of these different cultures as well as different disciplines. For instance, for a better understanding of classroom dynamics, aspects such as attitudes toward female teachers or methods used to teach history in different countries must be taken into account when analyzing responses.

Methodology

To assess the newly designed courses taught in fall 2017 and receive feedback about the overall experience, the ILC developed an eleven-question online survey via SurveyMonkey. Participants answered nine open-ended questions (appendix 2B) designed to gather qualitative feedback on teaching experiences, student learning and assessment, incorporation of the ACRL *Framework for Information Literacy for Higher Education*, course design successes and challenges, areas for improvement, and cultural implications.[4] Questions ten and eleven supplied demographic data.

The online survey, reviewed by the ILC and the workshop leaders, Samantha Godbey and Xan Goodman, was e-mailed twice in spring 2018 to all twenty-eight participants from the 2017 Paris workshop. A reminder to complete the survey was announced during an online meeting with all co-designers prior to the survey closing deadline. One team of co-designers opted not to participate in the survey because they were not available to teach the pilot course in fall 2017. Out of twenty-six potential respondents, fourteen replied to the survey: seven faculty members and seven librarians.

It should be pointed out that the survey was developed by the ILC members, four of whom attended the workshop and also participated in the survey as respondents. The content analysis of the survey responses was conducted by the five members of the ILC, the authors of this chapter. In order to reduce the risk of subjectivity, each was assigned random questions from the survey to analyze, which they aggregated by themes and patterns revealed by the survey responses before the contributions were reviewed by their peers.

To analyze the results, we used a summative content approach that recognizes themes and patterns in order to explore a deeper meaning, while "identifying and quantifying certain words or content in text with the purpose of understanding the contextual use of the words or content."[5] This method of analysis follows the tradition of "thick description" by Geertz and Ryle,[6] where meaning and credibility of interpretation are achieved by a "thickness of description."[7]

Survey Results

A first review of the data brought to light mostly positive feedback about the co-design experience. "The library sessions went well!" (Faculty 14) and "Library sessions went perfectly well throughout the entire Fall session 2017" (Librarian 2) summarize the general reaction to the co-designing experience for both faculty and librarians, although not all experiences were a success. One librarian said, "Armed by the knowledge gained from the Paris IL training workshop… we reviewed the entire course syllabus; discussed classroom expectations; and redesigned the class around a new teaching paradigm…. Based on [the ACRL Framework], we redrafted the course syllabus, revamped the library information literacy workshops, and produced a new course syllabus" (Librarian 2). The word *together* was mentioned several times to highlight how the experience was conducive to collaborative practices: "The workshop was a first opportunity to dialog and spend time together reflecting on the new course" (Librarian 4). Librarians reported being satisfied with the chance to co-teach with faculty and have an impact on a course; faculty were happy to rely on the librarians' knowledge in guiding and helping students with specific assignments: "The library sessions went smoothly" (Faculty 6) and "The sessions went really well, as students were interested and cooperative" (Librarian 8).

Another faculty member echoed the positive impact of the workshop on the instructional design by linking it to students' *successful* learning. "The Co-Design workshop revolutionized my planning of the course. It was the first time I was teaching it and it was very successful because the students got a lot out of the project" (Faculty 11). Student learning and improvement of core skills were key to the co-design project. Even a faculty member who had previously taught the same course many times noted, "The students were receptive and many of their assignments reflected skills they learned during the library sessions.... Their research skills improved vastly. It should be said that before the Paris workshop, information literacy was not a major goal of the class. The main success is that [the students'] work improved" (Faculty 10).

Furthermore, students were "engaged" (Librarian 7), "interested" (Librarian 8), and "empowered" (Faculty 1 and 10) by the active and dynamic lessons. One significant quote that encapsulates the students' responses to newly developed teaching material states, "They thought that the bar was being raised in terms of the research requirements for each assignment, but they responded to the gauntlet and rose to the challenge. I now have some amazingly well-sourced and interdisciplinary essays as a result" (Faculty 3).

Course Redesign with the Framework

The newly co-designed courses represented a variety of disciplines, including comparative literature, gender studies, communications, history, writing, and business. Most of the courses were introductory courses or first-year experiences. Survey respondents saw the disciplinary course content and the ACRL Framework as two pieces of the same puzzle. One faculty member stated, "Now that we have incorporated it into the class, it seems like *a perfect fit*" (Faculty 10), and a librarian echoed almost the same words: "Information literacy components seemed to *perfectly fit* into enhancing the ...learning process" (Librarian 2). Another librarian said that the frame "[Information Creation as a Process] comes along naturally to the ...course" (Librarian 12).

Collaboration brought to each new course a structure that better integrates information literacy concepts, which are addressed in scaffolded sessions and subsequently become "more focused" (Faculty 10). Most respondents provided enthusiastic responses regarding the changes made after the workshop attendance. The various courses "integrated the changes" (Faculty 1) and the "strategies recommended during the workshop" (Librarian 7). They have been "substantially revamped and redesigned" (Librarian 2), with revised learning outcomes based on the six frames.

The frame most often mentioned by the co-designer teams was Scholarship as Conversation, with seven references, followed by Searching as Strategic Exploration and Research as Inquiry, with six references each. Authority Is Constructed and Contextual was mentioned five times, Information Creation as a Process four times, and Information Has Value three times. Overall, all respondents mentioned the application of more than one frame in their co-designed courses. One faculty member also said that they "touched on all Frames" (Faculty 10).

One faculty member, however, noted that assignments from the librarian did not carry much weight for the students. Many times those assignments are not graded, and therefore the students do not take them seriously. This faculty member stated, "Students didn't pay any special attention to the librarian's assignments which were ungraded.... Students generally ignore ungraded assignments, but when they found out that they are graded alongside the course assignments, they paid more attention to them" (Faculty 6). A librarian shared this opinion: "The faculty's comments were even more effective and heard as they do the grading. The role of librarian is not seen as somebody who is grading students' work" (Librarian 12).

Several respondents agreed on the value of the library instruction, including students' positive image of the library as a place of research and also the recognition that a librarian can have an important role in course design. One co-designer mentioned that through "end of semester reflections" (Faculty 6) students intimated that they were able to transfer and apply information literacy concepts to other courses.

Assignment Design

A great variety of assignments were used in the co-designed courses. Among them stood out assignments such as book and film reviews, which required the critical use of library online journals; evaluation of peer-reviewed and non-peer-reviewed articles; and open-ended papers for research reflection. Faculty also relied on standard assignments such as annotated bibliographies, search logs, and in-class process writing. One respondent added that the graded reference lists made a difference to their teaching as it helped both highlight mistakes and offer suggestions on how to improve. Students were encouraged to be more independent through in-class guidance and independent work on assignments.

During the pilot courses, the librarians worked with different assignments to check student understanding. Undeniably, the purpose of all the implemented learning strategies, exercises, and tasks was to determine if students understood what resources to use and to help students develop their information literacy competencies, or more precisely their research and critical-thinking skills, in the context of the frames. Most of the library sessions made use of active learning exercises, including Background Knowledge Probe, memory matrix, comparative book reviews, Content Form and Function Outlines, and the writing of blog posts.

Assessment

A crucial part of the learning process was assessing and summarizing the effect of the organized training sessions on students' understanding of the concepts discussed. All the survey respondents showed great creativity in the means used for assessing students' knowledge, other than using the popular one-minute paper.

Many of the librarians expressed satisfaction with being involved in defining assessment criteria and evaluation processes, though this remains primarily a faculty area of expertise. The librarians involved in the pilot courses used various types of formative assessment to evaluate student performance during the library sessions. Most of the librarians agreed that the so-called on-the-spot assessment (or instant feedback assessment) seemed to be the most effective tool for assessing students' learning progress during the co-designed courses because it gave real insights into the practical skills acquired by the students.

Cultural Implications of the Frames

Among all participants, only eleven respondents answered the question related to the cultural implications of the ACRL frames. These answers did not provide clear insight about possible implications of applying the frames in instructional contexts different from the United States. Although the majority of the respondents did not notice any cultural implications resulting from the specific instructional context, we can indicate some connections between the cultural context and the application of the frames.

Recurring survey responses highlighted that differences in educational background between US and international students may affect how students receive and perceive the concepts embedded in the Framework. Some threshold concepts are more challenging both for the instructors to address and for the students to grasp due to explicit cultural differences. One librarian summed up the situation, saying, "Learning styles based on memorization rather than inquiry and critical thinking impacted the pace of the course" (Librarian 6).

One respondent noticed that cultural differences come up when students are free to choose their research topic. In other words, the choice of a topic is often dictated by their own cultural background, but this does not necessarily influence the use of the frames. One more instance in which cultural differences play an important role is when broad issues are discussed. For example, one faculty respondent noticed, "It was clear that depending on country of origin, students have different perceptions of fake news" (Faculty 10). Another respondent clearly indicated that students' English proficiency level was one of the biggest barriers to applying the frames and a crucial factor in their performance in the courses (Librarian 6).

The survey responses did not clearly indicate whether the cultural background of an institution and its faculty, librarians, and students shapes how the frames are approached. Some comments seemed to go in this direction, but it was not possible to affirm with absolute certainty that cultural background plays a role in student learning within this context.

Future Implications

The librarian-faculty collaborative relationship must strike a delicate balance in order to become established and flourish. Char Booth and colleagues described these faculty-librarian partnerships as key to successful instruction.[8] For the co-design workshop experience, collaboration was an intentional requirement for participation. All respondents provided interesting feedback about how to further improve their collaboration and presented new ideas and projects that they are already considering for future iterations of the courses. For example, one faculty member stated, “We take from this to increase library sessions in the future and to have special tutorials for students who are struggling. We will also attempt to better assess their learning in the future” (Faculty 13).

Several respondents, although emphasizing the positive aspects of the experience, pointed out that these collaborations remain a work in progress, and they all described how they were planning to reorganize their way of integrating the library into course assignments.

Other suggestions for future improvement include consistent planning as a means of achieving better results for their students. Similar collaborations require that the faculty member and the librarian spend time together coordinating library instruction with class assignments. As one librarian noted, “I hope we will meet before the course and set up what to do between three of us and not come up ‘on the spot’ with a plan of what to do that day. I want to go back through the notes and include the third professor and work on creating a cohesive group project” (Librarian 5).

Conclusion

The overall results of the survey provide positive feedback on the collaborative experiences that were piloted in fall 2017, signifying that both faculty and librarians saw improvements over the practices to which they were accustomed. Faculty members expressed their approval of the projects, while librarians highlighted the positive impact of in-depth collaboration with faculty on their instruction. One respondent said, “Thinking with the frameworks has given me more confidence on where we need to go with our students, although I am not necessarily teaching all of the frames” (Librarian 4). Another respondent stated, “The idea of research as discovery is now fundamental to my understanding of information literacy, and a concept I have tried to systematically share with my students this semester” (Faculty 3).

Threshold concepts and the frames are seen as effective tools that can definitely help improve information literacy integration in other courses as well, as long as they are made relevant to the students so they understand how these concepts can be applied in everyday life.

Faculty members remain responsible for developing course assignments, and therefore librarians still do not have the opportunity to take part in the assessment of student progress as much as they would like. The challenge for librarians here is to have an impact on student learning in the absence of grading. It is possible to argue that crossing thresholds motivates and engages students to move beyond short-term goals such as grades, credits, and diplomas into deeper learning, which helps develop the critical-thinking skills that support and enhance lifelong learning. While the majority of survey respondents confirmed that the graded assignment is still perceived as a faculty-only privilege, perhaps this is an inroad toward which librarians can work.

Although the survey aimed to analyze the co-design experience in its entirety, some issues were not addressed by the respondents. Despite the positive reactions to the assessment methods introduced in the workshop, one concern remains: the difficulty of assessing threshold concepts, especially because the internalization of these concepts needs to happen over time and not be limited to a single instruction session.[9] However, the conceptual teaching of the threshold concepts within these co-designed courses is limited to an introduction to the ACRL Framework, which must be revisited in later reiterations. One faculty member extended this idea by saying that what matters is the transformation of student research habits in the long term.

Another issue that could not be addressed by the survey is whether assessment of the threshold concepts rests solely with the faculty member, the librarian, or both in order to create a joint effort in correlating these complex concepts within the disciplinary learning outcomes. The co-design workshop attempted to unify faculty and librarian expertise so as to join forces for assignment design and assessment for the sake of student learning.

Finally, although some respondents noted students' positive reactions to the faculty-librarian collaboration, the survey results do not reveal student perceptions. An in-depth analysis of student perspectives may be warranted for future study in order to develop a comprehensive picture of how similar collaborative projects might influence student academic performance and retention of the fundamental concepts highlighted by the frames.

Spanning a variety of disciplines, including communications, business, and comparative literature, the majority of the co-designed projects targeted freshmen and involved an extensive writing component. This helped reveal directions in which successful faculty-librarian partnerships may prosper. As Mader suggested, "The ACRL Framework has created a lingua franca for common conversation between librarians and writing instructors."[10] In other words, the

Framework speaks a language that librarians can easily share with faculty,[11] introducing common themes and concepts that become natural starting points for possible collaborations. The six frames identify concepts that are already integrated in the teaching, which makes the collaboration with librarians easier to establish. On a deeper collaborative level, faculty-librarian partnership can also involve curriculum development.[12] This can easily happen within general education committees in which librarians already collaborate with faculty. Nevertheless, the co-design experience demonstrates that there can be some misunderstanding about how the Framework should be used and integrated in course development. The case studies in this volume based on the co-design experience show how developing a deeper collaboration between faculty and librarians can improve both faculty-librarian partnerships and student learning.

APPENDIX 2A

List of Participating Institutions

Al Akhawayn University in Ifrane, Morocco
American University in Bulgaria
American University of Armenia
American University of Beirut, Lebanon
American University of Central Asia, Kyrgyzstan
American University of Kosovo
American University of Kuwait
American University of Paris, France
American University of Sharjah, United Arab Emirates
Franklin University, Switzerland
John Cabot University, Italy

APPENDIX 2B

Survey Questions

1. **Describe:** Describe your co-designed course (taught in Fall 2017). Feel free to email the syllabus to us.
2. **Librarian sessions:** How did the library sessions work out? Which ACRL Frame did you include into your instruction as your learning outcome? How many times did the librarians intervene?
3. **Change:** To what extent did you include changes during the workshop to the initial course that you brought to the Paris workshop? Any change the workshop provoked in your instructional thinking or practice?
4. **Reflect:** Reflect on your teaching experience of the co-designed course. What were challenges and success stories (lessons learned)?
5. **Students:** How did the students do in the co-designed course? How did they respond to the teaching material this semester?
6. **Assignments and assessment:** What assignments and forms of assessment of student learning did you find most effective with regard to the co-designed course?
7. **Learning activities:** What learning activities or approaches did you find particularly effective?
8. **Cultural implications of the ACRL Frames:** Do you have any comments about cultural implications of the Frames as applied in your instructional contexts?
9. **Improvement:** What can be improved for next time? What will you keep or apply to other courses? Did you come up with a new idea or a new project?

Notes

1. Thomas A. Angelo, "Doing Assessment as if Learning Matters Most: Three Steps to Transformative Practice," *AAHE Bulletin* 51, no. 9 (1999): 3–6.
2. Samantha Godbey and Xan Goodman, "Co-design: Integrating Information Literacy into Your Disciplinary Course" (AMICAL workshop, American University of Paris, March 31–April 1, 2017), https://www.amicalnet.org/events/co-design-integrating-information-literacy-into-your-disciplinary-course.

3. Clifford Geertz, *The Interpretation of Cultures* (New York: Basic Books, 1973).
4. Association of College and Research Libraries, *Framework for Information Literacy for Higher Education* (Chicago: Association of College and Research Libraries, 2016).
5. Hsiu-Fang Hsieh and Sarah E. Shannon, "Three Approaches to Qualitative Content Analysis," *Qualitative Health Research* 15, no. 9 (2005): 1283, https://doi.org/10.1177/1049732305276687.
6. Geertz, *Interpretation of Cultures*; Gilbert Ryle, *Collected Papers* (London: Routledge, 2009).
7. Joseph Ponterotto, "Brief Note on the Origins, Evolution, and Meaning of the Qualitative Research Concept Thick Description," *Qualitative Report* 11, no. 3 (2006): 543.
8. Char Booth et al., "Degrees of Impact: Analyzing the Effects of Progressive Librarian Course Collaborations on Student Performance," *College and Research Libraries* 76, no. 5 (2015): 623–51, https://doi.org/10.5860/crl.76.5.623.
9. Jan H. F. Meyer and Ray Land, *Threshold Concepts and Troublesome Knowledge*, Occasional Report 4 (Edinburgh, UK: Enhancing Teaching-Learning Environments in Undergraduate Courses Project, 2003), http://www.leeds.ac.uk/educol/documents/142206.pdf.
10. Sharon Mader, "Foreword," in *Rewired: Research-Writing Partnerships within the Frameworks*, ed. Randall McClure (Chicago: Association of College and Research Libraries, 2016), v.
11. LuMarie F. Guth et al., "Faculty Voices on the Framework: Implications for Instruction and Dialogue," *portal: Libraries and the Academy* 18, no. 4 (2018): 693–718, https://doi.org/10.1353/pla.2018.0041.
12. Kacy Lundstrom, Britt Anna Fagerheim, and Elizabeth Benson, "Librarians and Instructors Developing Student Learning Outcomes: Using Frameworks to Lead the Process," *Reference Services Review* 42, no. 3 (2014): 484–98, https://doi.org/10.1108/RSR-04-2014-0007.

Bibliography

Angelo, Thomas A. "Doing Assessment as if Learning Matters Most: Three Steps to Transformative Practice." *AAHE Bulletin* 51, no. 9 (1999): 3–6.

Association of College and Research Libraries. *Framework for Information Literacy for Higher Education*. Chicago: Association of College and Research Libraries, 2016.

Booth, Char M., Sara Lowe, Natalie Tagge, and Sean M. Stone. "Degrees of Impact: Analyzing the Effects of Progressive Librarian Course Collaborations on Student Performance." *College and Research Libraries* 76, no. 5 (2015): 623–51. https://doi.org/10.5860/crl.76.5.623.

Geertz, Clifford. *The Interpretation of Cultures: Selected Essays*. New York: Basic Books, 1973.

Godbey, Samantha, and Xan Goodman. "Co-design: Integrating Information Literacy into Your Disciplinary Course." AMICAL workshop, American University of Paris, March 31–April 1, 2017. https://www.amicalnet.org/events/co-design-integrating-information-literacy-into-your-disciplinary-course.

Guth, LuMarie F., Judith M. Arnold, Veronica E. Bielat, Maria A. Perez-Stable, and Patricia Fravel Vander Meer. "Faculty Voices on the Framework: Implications for Instruction and Dialogue." *portal: Libraries and the Academy* 18, no. 4 (2018): 693–718. https://doi.org/10.1353/pla.2018.0041.

Hsieh, Hsiu-Fang, and Sarah E. Shannon. "Three Approaches to Qualitative Content Analysis." *Qualitative Health Research* 15, no. 9 (2005): 1277–88. https://doi.org/10.1177/1049732305276687.

Lundstrom, Kacy, Britt Anna Fagerheim, and Elizabeth Benson. "Librarians and Instructors Developing Student Learning Outcomes: Using Frameworks to Lead the Process." *Reference Services Review* 42, no. 3 (2014): 484–98. https://doi.org/10.1108/RSR-04-2014-0007.

Mader, Sharon. "Foreword." in *Rewired: Research-Writing Partnerships within the Frameworks.* Edited by Randall McClure, v-vii. Chicago: Association of College and Research Libraries, 2016.

Meyer, Jan H. F., and Ray Land. *Threshold Concepts and Troublesome Knowledge: Linkages to Ways of Thinking and Practicing*, Occasional Report 4. Edinburgh, UK: Enhancing Teaching-Learning Environments in Undergraduate Courses Project, 2003. http://www.leeds.ac.uk/educol/documents/142206.pdf.

Ponterotto, Joseph. "Brief Note on the Origins, Evolution, and Meaning of the Qualitative Research Concept Thick Description." *Qualitative Report* 11, no. 3 (2006): 538–49.

Ryle, Gilbert. *Collected Papers.* London: Routledge, 2009.

SECTION II
Case Studies

CASE STUDY 1

Revising the Syllabus

Integrating Information Literacy into a General Education History Course at Al Akhawayn University in Ifrane, Morocco

Paul M. Love, Jr.

Assistant Professor of North African, Middle Eastern, and Islamic History, Al Akhawayn University, Ifrane, Morocco

Aziz El Hassani

Researcher and Learning Services Supervisor, Mohammed VI Library, Al Akhawayn University, Ifrane, Morocco

Introduction: Why a History Class?

The following book chapter describes an information literacy (IL) integration initiative at Al Akhawayn University in Ifrane (AUI) as successful through faculty-librarian collaboration and discusses how it can be embedded into an existing general education curriculum. When planning this collaborative project to integrate IL into the curriculum at our university, we chose a course entitled History of the Arab World. We chose this course for a variety of reasons, including those related to the university general education curriculum and also for reasons specific to the course content. As for the first, this particular course is one of two options for a history course requirement for all students in the university, regardless of their major or educational background. As such, the course carried the potential to expose a maximum number of students to IL during our pilot project. Students take this course anytime between their first and last years at the university, which further diversified our sample. Moreover, the focal objective of the coursework requires students to understand the ways in which reviews and interpretations of academic books vary according to the context (for example, the journal or publication in which the review appears) as well as the views and biases of the review's author.

In addition to the course introducing a large and diverse body of students to IL, we found that its content and discipline complemented well many of the IL goals we were interested in integrating into the curriculum. As a first-year history course—and often the only history course these students would take over their academic careers—this class introduces students to the history of the Arab world and to the discipline of history in general. Historians seek out information, analyze it, and deploy it in the form of telling a historical narrative and making an argument. Presenting the field in this way and using context-specific examples drawn from Arab history proved an excellent method for demonstrating the importance and application of information literacy.

Course Structure and Workshops as Complementary Tools for Teaching Information Literacy

We approached our pilot project together with the focal objective of enhancing the academic performance of students. We aimed at steering students' interest toward a new scholastic approach to studying the history of the Arab world while also helping students to develop the information literacy skills that could help them throughout their academic careers and beyond. The co-design approach gave us an ideal academic platform for collaboration, while the Association of College and Research Libraries' (ACRL) Framework for Information Literacy for Higher Education served as a point of departure and a road map toward advancing and reaching our common objective.[1]

Fall 2017 marked our first attempt to integrate IL into the curriculum at Al Akhawayn University, using the ACRL Framework as a guide. The Framework provided a robust opportunity for us (faculty member and librarian) to work closely in redesigning and embedding targeted IL skills into the course History of the Arab World. During our early co-design stage, the Framework served as both a guideline for planning and a conceptual reference point for mutual academic collaboration. From the librarian's perspective, our collaborative IL teaching experience has transformed the traditional AUI Library's IL workshops beyond merely finding information sources into more specialized training sessions with targeted outcomes that are immediately applicable to students.

As we redesigned the course with the goals of our collaboration in mind, we also sought to restructure it such that the library-based workshops and the existing course content could prove complementary to one another. We agreed that the course would have four information literacy instruction sessions throughout the fall 2017 semester. The objective was to gradually introduce students to the concept of information literacy and to buttress and reinforce the research skills gained from previous IL sessions. First and foremost, we offered a short workshop at the beginning of the semester in which the concept of information literacy and the ACRL Framework were introduced to the students. This was a general introduction offered by Aziz (the librarian). The discussion that followed was led by both Aziz and Paul (the faculty member); it asked students to draw possible connections between IL and the study of history.

Students were quick to identify parallels between them, which proved useful as we moved through the course because Paul could return to these basic principles of IL in a variety of contexts. In fact, many of the class sessions were restructured with the basic concepts of information literacy in mind. For example, Aziz introduced students in the opening workshop to the ACRL frame Scholarship as Conversation. In a later class session on medieval Spain, students examined two contradictory accounts of tolerance among religious communities there. Using a concrete example from history, students learned how two experts in the same scholarly field could come to entirely different conclusions about the past—even when using the same sources of information.

Later workshops were aimed more precisely at encouraging students to develop their own understanding of the IL concepts and ACRL frames. After they had seen several examples of Scholarship as Conversation, students went through workshops to help them prepare their midterm project, which was a comparative book review assignment. Students were asked to identify a scholarly history book on a topic of their choice and then to compare and contrast book reviews of that book. In the library workshops, Aziz helped students identify scholarly books by using IL to understand what makes an academic book different from other books (e.g., identifying the source of the information in the form of author, credentials, publisher, and so forth). These activities complemented similar exercises used by Paul in previous classes in which he had students do some quick research on the authors and publishers of the sources they were reading.

The next step was to identify academic reviews for their chosen book, for which Aziz offered a workshop on using tools on the library's website. Once students identified their books and obtained the reviews, they wrote a short narrative essay on how the similarities and differences among the reviews demonstrated the concept of Scholarship as Conversation.

A Final Project in IL: Revising the Syllabus

In an approach that was similar to the midterm project, we designed the final exam portion of the class as a final IL-based project in which students revised the syllabus. Each student identified a specific class session in the syllabus that they thought could be improved. Alternatively, students could expand a topic by adding an additional session or even introduce an entirely new topic. Regardless of their choice, they were asked to identify one to two ACRL frames for IL and demonstrate how their new class plan integrated the goals of these frames. Their class plans required a title, class goals, reading or other materials for students to prepare before class, and in-class activities. The goal was to determine whether the basic ideas of information literacy discussed in the previous library IL instructive sessions were processed and put into action. The details of this particular aspect are the topic of a separate publication.[2]

Many students did remarkable work for this assignment. One especially impressive class plan, which also did a great job integrating IL goals, was prepared by Ms. Kenza Soufiane, an engineering student.[3] Kenza's project focused on the development of stereotypes of Arabs in Anglophone comics and cartoons from the 1940s to the present. Her class plan included comic books, video clips, discussion questions, and a worksheet.

The lesson plan included three goals:

1. Discuss critically the use of comic books and cartoons as a means of producing stereotypes and creating propaganda.

2. Compare the current representations of Arabs to the ones in the mid-twentieth century.
3. Discuss how the cartoons and comic books produced by Arabs for an Arab audience can enhance (or not) the stereotypes.

For these purposes, she chose a variety of examples of cartoons and comic books. One of the more striking examples was a short clip from a Looney Tunes cartoon from the 1940s in which the character Porky Pig was a member of the French Foreign Legion in North Africa and fought with a group of Arabs led by "Ali Baba, the Mad Dog of the Desert," which she had students contrast with another example from *The Simpsons* television show from the end of the twentieth century in which the Simpson family visits Marrakesh, Morocco.

By studying and discussing the shared stereotypes, Kenza's assignment sought to demonstrate to students the persistence and danger of stereotypes, as well as the importance of demonstrating how comics and cartoons can serve to propagate them. Kenza's choice of cartoons was very well thought out, since the Looney Tunes cartoon was set in World War Two–era northern Africa, which was a historical setting on which we spent an entire week earlier in the course. *The Simpsons* cartoon was set in an even more familiar environment, since most of our students are Moroccan and some are themselves from Marrakesh. The chance to explore stereotypes in cartoons set in familiar locations made the exercise in IL one to which many students felt personally connected.

Kenza explained the rationale behind her choice of this particular topic within the context of an assignment that pushed students to engage with information literacy in the following way:

> *This lesson plan achieves Information Creation as a Process as an ACRL frame for information literacy. Information in general, is created to pass on a message and is shared by different means such as media, the internet, stories, cartoons, books, comics, and documentaries. Preconceived ideas about Arabs were not constructed by chance. They are the product and the consequence of the usage of many methods of propaganda over a long period of time. The process of creating misleading information about Arabs is not recent, as the comparison between the images shown in the early 40's and those shown in the present-day share a theme about the Arabs. Despite all*

> *the technology, and the development of several countries of the Arab world may have witnessed, the image depicted remains the same for more than 50 years, as if time had stopped for the Arabs....*
>
> *Indeed, how the Arabs are perceived by the world is a process that not only started a long time ago, but also targeted individuals of different ages. And that process follows individuals as they grow. Thus, this lesson plan achieves Information Creation as a Process as an ACRL frame for information literacy, not only by [showing] how ...information... [has been produced] over the years ...but also by exhibiting how the information creation process has molded individuals' brains, regardless of their ages, and substantially framed their perspectives ([f]rom cartoons to media, the representation of Arabs is the same).*[4]

Conclusion

This chapter has highlighted the importance of faculty-librarian collaborative projects in achieving integration of information literacy, which almost by default enhances students' learning and research skills. We believe that our collaboration achieved its intended learning goals and was successfully applied to most of the components of the course History of the Arab World. The embedded IL workshops allowed significant involvement of students in academic research and creative scholarly activities, ultimately having them produce concrete examples and plans for how to integrate further IL components into the course. The choice to collaborate on integrating IL into a general education course enhanced our ability to reach the maximum number of students possible.

We gained a lot from this academic collaborative journey, and we plan to collaborate in the future, both on embedding ACRL's *Framework for Information Literacy for Higher Education* into core curriculum as discussed here and other similar initiatives. For AUI Library, we believe that this case study succeeded in adding an initial opportunity to consider establishing future information literacy learning outcomes and measurable assessment tools based on the ACRL Framework. The goal is to augment students' information literacy competency skills and initiate more faculty-librarian collaborations. Such collaborative initiatives have always benefited students in terms of acquiring quality information literacy skills education, produced better embedding of librarians in university academic units, and brought about more faculty awareness of library resources and services.

Notes

1. Association of College and Research Libraries, *Framework for Information Literacy for Higher Education* (Chicago: Association of College and Research Libraries, 2016), 3, http://www.ala.org/acrl/sites/ala.org.acrl/files/content/issues/infolit/Framework_ILHE.pdf.
2. Aziz El Hassani, "Embedding Information Literacy into a Humanities Course Using the ACRL Framework as a Guide: A Faculty-Librarian Collaboration Model," in *Library Partnerships in International Library Arts Education*, ed. Jeff Hiroshi Gima and Kara Malenfant (Chicago: Association of College and Research Libraries, forthcoming).
3. Kenza Soufiane, "How Has the Image of the Arabs Depicted in Comics and Cartoons Been Changing over the Years?" (final project report, HIS1301 History of the Arab World, Al Akhawayn University, 2017). The details of and quotations from Kenza's project are used with her permission. Many thanks to her for both her original work and her willingness to share it with others in this chapter.
4. Soufiane, "How Has the Image of the Arabs?"

Bibliography

Association of College and Research Libraries. *Framework for Information Literacy for Higher Education*. Chicago: Association of College and Research Libraries, 2016. http://www.ala.org/acrl/sites/ala.org.acrl/files/content/issues/infolit/Framework_ILHE.pdf.

El Hassani, Aziz. "Embedding Information Literacy into a Humanities Course Using the ACRL Framework as a Guide: A Faculty-Librarian Collaboration Model." In *Library Partnerships in International Library Arts Education*. Edited by Jeff Hiroshi Gima and Kara Malenfant. Chicago: Association of College and Research Libraries, forthcoming.

Soufiane, Kenza. "How Has the Image of the Arabs Depicted in Comics and Cartoons Been Changing over the Years?" Final project report, HIS1301 History of the Arab World, Al Akhawayn University, 2017.

Vrchota, Denise. "Touchstone Award: Challenging Students' Thinking with Bloom's 'Taxonomy.'" *Communication Teacher* 18, no.1 (2004): 2–5.

CASE STUDY 2

Developing Marketing Plans and the Beauty of Research

Meaghan Scott Seyve

Lecturer, International Business Department, American University of Paris, France

Michael Stöpel

User Services Librarian, American University of Paris, France

Introduction

Identifying credible sources, according to Wineburg and McGrew, is a complicated issue in today's information landscape.[1] This is even more important given that there is more information available at our fingertips than in the past. Confronting this situation, students need to become more skillful and knowledgeable in order to do well: they need to have knowledge about databases, websites, and other places of knowledge where they can find reliable information; they need to know how to identify markers of quality, such as peer-reviewed journals or trustworthy places of knowledge in the field such as the marketing course discussed in this chapter; they need skills and experience to navigate these sources of knowledge, using basic ideas of *smart searching*, truncation, filtering results, and modifying search queries to render the initial searches more effective. These imply an attitude of *informed skepticism*, an anti-*hubristic attitude*, as Wineburg and McGrew called it, in order to approach information critically and to evaluate its academic quality and relevancy.

In the course Marketing in a Global Environment, the student assignment is to develop authentic marketing plans and presentations by applying the content of the course textbook. After being assigned to teams with diverse skills using the IDEO Ten Faces of Innovation Method,[2] students then brainstorm a need or identify a void in the French marketplace. To solve this problem, students create a business idea, learn to do marketing research, and build a plan to bring their idea into the French market. The student teams learn how to market different products or services of their choice step-by-step through the chapters in their textbook. Giving the students the power to choose what they want to focus on brings more passion to the research and understanding of the customer. Authentic marketing plans and presentations are the structuring elements of the course, as students prepare and present them three times during the semester—after week 3, during midterms, and during final exams.

We apply the textbook in a practical way so that students' understanding of macro- and microenvironment comes from concrete experience. This approach helps students understand marketing and how to research the macro environment using primary and secondary data for a product or service they have created. Conducting research helps students to work together and to make marketing decisions as an empowered team.

From a discipline-specific perspective, prior to the faculty-librarian collaboration, student presentations were not as deeply rooted in customer research databases. Students conducted surveys in person and online to gather customer insights. But they could not answer questions about trends in the marketplace and the demographics of a potential customer base. Their marketing plans needed better-sourced data to be realistic and fact-checkable. Library databases are valuable resources that many students did not utilize in their research methods before the co-design of this course.

Co-designing

The Paris co-design workshop caused us to rethink and co-design the course content for our instruction.[3] We started off by identifying the most common student bottlenecks in class and defining learning outcomes that would match frames in the ACRL *Framework for Information Literacy for Higher Education*.[4]

Coming into the course, the librarian realized that students struggled to find trustful sources to support their arguments, use in-text citation for information (and images) in a proper way, and to create works cited lists correctly. For the faculty member, another important bottleneck was student inability to develop arguments based on reliable sources.

We saw early in the process that core concepts in both academic fields, marketing and information literacy, are closely related to each other or overlap with regard to common educational goals. In both fields, the frames Information Creation as a Process and Authority Is Constructed and Contextual are central learning outcomes. The two frames are linked to the bottlenecks in the sense that understanding of authority and the information creation process lead to a better analysis of statistics. These were the starting points to improve students' marketing plans and their presentations.

An advantage was that we knew each other already. For example, we had well-established ways of communicating with each other, we had experience co-teaching, and we knew that our ways of teaching were well-matched: doing marketing and doing research. In other words, both pedagogies, doing research and writing a marketing plan, were embedded in a learning-by-doing approach. This matching aspect facilitated the co-teaching and integration of information literacy into the marketing course.

From the Bottleneck to Embedded Research Sessions

As a result of the workshop, we modified various aspects of our already existing collaboration (see table CS2.1). We added library sessions and set up various opportunities to give direct and formative feedback to students focused specifically on bottlenecks. A major aspect of the co-designed course was to set up two research sessions instead of one. Both library sessions were held in the regular marketing classroom and were labeled as research sessions. They were taught before the first group of presentations. By implementing an added library session, our thinking was to combine elements of marketing instruction and library instruction. For example, in the first library session, we set up a short survey for students. The survey was based on the idea of collecting data about the students' previous knowledge regarding research and their confidence doing research.[5] The pre-knowledge student survey activity allowed us to echo it with a post-assessment at the end of the semester.

At the same time, one task in the marketing course was for students to design a marketing survey in order to research their target market. In a nutshell, the objective of the pre-knowledge student survey was three-fold.

Table CS2.1

Overview of embedded library sessions and elements before and after the co-design workshop

From Collaboration to Co-design			
Fall 2016: BEFORE	***Spring 2017: BEFORE***	***Summer 2017: AFTER***	***Summer 2018: AFTER***
1st library research sessions	1st library research sessions	1st co-designed library research sessions	1st improved co-designed library research sessions
		2nd co-designed library research sessions	2nd improved co-designed library research sessions
		Librarian attending and commenting on the 1st group presentations	Librarian attending and commenting on the 1st group presentations
		Group-specific feedback directly in the online group presentation slides (i.e., Google Slides)	Group-specific feedback directly in the online group presentation slides (i.e., Google Slides)
		Drop-in session in person giving feedback on most common issues in the group presentation slides	Drop-in session in person giving feedback on most common issues in the group presentation slides
	Collective e-mail pointing out common issues in the group presentation slides	Collective e-mail pointing out common issues in the group presentation slides	Collective e-mail pointing out common issues in the group presentation slides

From Collaboration to Co-design			
Fall 2016: BEFORE	***Spring 2017: BEFORE***	***Summer 2017: AFTER***	***Summer 2018: AFTER***
		Librarian attending the final group presentations	Librarian attending the final group presentations with the start-up company
			Faculty member asked for input on grading

First, students themselves experienced the data production circle and the consumer perspective, jump-starting reflections on the concept of Information Creation as a Process as well as Authority Is Constructed and Contextual; second, the instructor learned about the students' prior knowledge and assumptions; finally, students gained experience with a survey, which is a real marketing research tool.

Another valuable feature was that we provided opportunities to give direct and formative feedback to students. This happened in various ways: (1) direct feedback immediately after the presentations; (2) feedback before the second presentations in the form of a short classroom visit where we pointed out low points and highlights of the first presentations; and (3) shared online slides in order to give direct feedback on team presentation slides:

1. After the co-design workshop, the marketing instructors invited the librarian to attend the student presentations and to give direct feedback highlighting the good and not-so-good aspects of their presentations, as explained later in the section "You Are the Jury." This change was very important because the librarian could directly see how students would use research in their work and could comment directly after the presentations.
2. Having taken notes during the first round of presentations, the librarian clustered the most important problems students encountered and the highlights of their presentations. The librarian used them in a follow-up drop-in session before the second round of presentations.

3. Equally important was the mandatory set-up of google slides in order to share their presentations. Using Google Slides allowed the faculty member and librarian to check in on their work and give instant feedback on the slides. This kind of feedback helped the instructors to observe the students' learning process asynchronously—to sit beside them virtually—and to help students sharpen their next presentation.

Doing Content

In the area of content, what matters is that both pedagogies, the marketing course pedagogy and the research sessions pedagogy, matched well. The library sessions were driven by the idea of engaging students in active learning during class. For instance, because students tested products that had been marketed, completed surveys, conducted surveys with product beta testers, were part of a jury, or did presentations of their marketing plans, they were performing and learning at the same time. The overlap of content and activities made instruction and learning more meaningful to the students.

Being Surveyed and Surveying

By having students participate in a survey and learn about basic elements of surveying, the instructors got students to start thinking about understanding gathering data and analyzing data sets. After conducting the entrance survey, the librarian would ask and discuss questions related to issues such as sampling bias, question bias, and response rate. Students would take more time to analyze statistics and the ways surveys are produced by digging deeper into the information creation details. In short, they would start to grasp the concept of Information Creation as a Process and hence evaluate, select, and value sources more carefully and critically for their assignments. The idea was that students, by completing a survey, construct knowledge and reflect on it in order to raise awareness.

Research Labs

Another example of learning by doing was a team searching activity in the second part of the library research sessions. After having created Google

Slides for their presentations, students were asked to research their topics in teams (called "research labs") and to collect sources and information on their team presentation slides. By checking in, the faculty member and the librarian gave input on sources and how they could be integrated into the marketing plan. The students would have to rate the value of sources used, and, as an intended side effect, the team searching activity resulted in peer learning. Students expressed a disposition of openness in working with and learning from each other.

You Are the Jury—A Co-designed Rubric

In order to assess if students would achieve the set learning outcomes, we co-designed a rubric—entitled You Are the Jury—for the team presentations focused on the bottlenecks of quality of sources, in-text citations, and bibliographies. At the second research session, we started by handing out the rubric, explaining to the students that we would use it to give feedback and grade their group presentations. After a short explanation of the rubric, we asked students to use the rubric themselves and to be the jury, judging previous student marketing presentations. We showed them two presentations of different academic value for five minutes each. Then, in a classic Think-Pair-Share setup, we asked them to silently fill in the rubric and then share their comments with another student before reporting out to the class. The aim was to raise students' awareness of how a presentation might look, to set standards, and to discuss and clarify the three criteria of the rubric with regard to their presentations.

Clearly, the advantage of using the newly developed rubric was to outline the instructors' expectations for the students. In addition to learning by seeing good and bad presentations, students articulated their feedback using the rubric (and the specific terms) to their peers. Naturally, students posed questions about what makes a good presentation and a bad presentation, which is seen as evidence of learning in action.

Last but not least, the activity You Are the Jury was highly effective as it was closely linked to the assignment and came at a teachable moment.[6] Teachable moments are those moments when students are receptive to the learning material. For example, a teachable moment occurs when students are researching statistics for their projects and a librarian intervenes at that moment to teach a statistical database.

Summer 2018

In the summer semester of 2018, which is a three-week intensive class, the instructional context changed in one significant aspect compared to our regular fourteen-week semester co-design. The faculty member had the opportunity to invite people from a start-up company to class to introduce themselves and their virtual reality (VR) product. The company asked students to develop a marketing plan for this endeavor. It tested its product on American University of Paris students and faculty outside the marketing class with the help of students in the marketing course. Students surveyed each beta tester after they tested the VR product. Conducting survey research helped the students to define the problems that a potential consumer might have and to measure the potential interest level in the market. From the research, the company found a major problem in customer use that forced it to redesign in its product. The students also used the primary data to establish changes in its marketing strategy. This course not only helped the students gain a real-life business perspective, but it also helped the start-up company distinguish critical areas where it needed improvement. Each student team created a different marketing presentation geared toward the target market they chose after researching the primary and secondary data from the library. The start-up company came to the final presentations to see three different strategies, to ask questions, and to give real feedback to the students. In the end, it chose the marketing strategy it felt was most convincing. Because the change in instructional context (having the VR company) was linked to the applicable frames, the frames became real in the classroom.

As an unintended side effect, another ACRL frame came up during instruction: Information Has Value. The question involved how to use information ethically, avoiding copyright infringement and using images legally.* The VR company had found images online and used them in its marketing activities. It was contacted by the company that owned the images and was asked to delete the images from its product description in order to avoid being sued. By hearing this real-life anecdote, students realized that their projects and research behavior were potentially exposed to heavy financial sanctions and consequences. The faculty member and the librarian, without having planned to do so, had included another ACRL frame.

* Association of College and Research Libraries, *Framework for Information Literacy for Higher Education* (Chicago: Association of College and Research Libraries, 2016), 6.

Reflections on Co-design and Au-délà

The co-designed teaching experiences in summer 2017, fall 2017, and summer 2018 were very satisfying to both the faculty member and the librarian. Both instructors brought their expertise to the classroom in order to establish academic standards in their fields of expertise and to raise the students' level of learning. Students' research skills, knowledge about sources, use of databases, and attitudes acknowledging the need for critical use of sources in presentations significantly improved, which is the overall aim of teaching.

From a business teacher's perspective, it was valuable to have a trained research specialist come into the classroom and talk about research methods in relation to the different projects. Each business idea and marketing presentation had its own set of research challenges. The students learned a lot from the other groups and built on that learning for the next presentation. Teachers have sets of skills and specializations that are different from those of librarians, and working together creates a better learning environment for the students. From a business teacher's perspective, I learned a lot about citations, new places to search for sources, and ways to support presentations in my professional life. Learning to create a superior marketing plan by understanding and developing deeper research methods learned from the librarian gave more value to this course than in previous years without the co-design.

Keeping teachers updated and interested in developing deeper areas of knowledge that complement their teaching skills and knowledge is crucial. After years of teaching and technological changes, it is important that teachers receive constant tech updates to keep up with their students and to maintain the competitiveness of the university. The university has exchange students from Silicon Valley and other high-tech areas where fifth graders are adept in coding and prototyping. Teachers and students benefit from being at least at the same technical level or from the teacher being at a level higher in their technological specialization.

From the librarian's perspective, it was interesting to see how the role of the librarian and the students' perceptions of librarians changed. For instance, the opportunity to see students' performances in real time and online enabled the librarian to give feedback and improve students' works instantly. The librarian, by doing so, was recognized as an instructor. In general this is not the case, especially when librarians are involved in one-shot sessions only. Head and Eisenberg's study underlines this fact. They say that students overlook librarians' research expertise.[7] For the students, the faculty member is key: the faculty member is seen as the main instructor and the person grading. Therefore, it is the value given by the main instructor to research that renders it important in the student projects. If students do not receive the message that the underlying research is important for a successful project, they will most likely not engage in serious research. In interviews with students about why they do not research, Stöpel highlighted those student comments.[8]

Lankes, the director of South Carolina's School of Library and Information Science and recipient of the American Library Association's 2016 Ken Haycock Award for Promoting Librarianship, brought up this idea of librarians' new roles in his book *Expect More.* He sees librarians as "proactive facilitator[s] of knowledge"[9]—facilitators in the sense that librarians are actively connecting to students when they work on projects and help them create new knowledge. Scott Bennett, Yale University librarian emeritus, joins Lankes in his call for a new librarianship and the role librarians should play in knowledge creation: "Academic libraries must no longer be understood primarily as agencies of information access, supporting institutional mission. They are now challenged to become agencies of learning meant to enact institutional mission."[10] Both authors argue that librarians should take on this role of knowledge facilitation and become involved in educational projects at universities and beyond—to make visible the librarians' added value to the university mission by shifting or adding priorities away from traditional simplified perceptions of libraries as book depositories or cataloging places and instead allow librarians to take an active part in students' learning projects. This change is significant with regard to students' perceptions of librarians.

Thinking about high impact on student learning, the question of assignment matters. Summer 2018 was an eye-opening experience: the students were impressed not only by the real marketing plan development for a real start-up company, but also by the fact that the company almost got sued for unethical use of images. These real-life experiences clearly caught the students' attention and had a high impact on their learning. During the final group discussions at the end of the summer course, students confirmed that it is highly important for them to see the link between the coursework and the real world. They said that developing a real marketing plan for the VR company was much more motivating than composing a paper that seemed to them an artificial exercise without a meaningful link to the real world.

Another question to reflect on is that co-designing does not necessarily mean a formal and long-term integration of information literacy concepts into teaching. To be fully integrated and recognized by faculty, the department, and the university, the co-designed learning experiences have to be validated in department meetings and various committees, such as curriculum committees. How and where the curriculum integration then starts depends on many factors. There are many sustainable inroads into the curriculum: they can be initiated top-down, such as by the Rowan University Information Literacy Task Force,[11] they can be generated bottom-up by library-friendly academic champions who promote information literacy,[12] or they can begin simply because of the fact that a culture of information literacy exists at an institution—"the way of life at our organization," as McGuiness puts it.[13] In all three approaches, the role of faculty members is crucial as they are the vectors of the educational project.[14]

Further on, the syllabus and learning outcomes frame the course content, but the way the class is taught belongs to the faculty member. The instructional pedagogy can vary from one collaborator or faculty member to another, and marketing and information literacy can be taught in many ways. It frequently happens that from one semester to the next, one of the collaborators who is teaching a course moves on to other courses or even another institution, changing the nature of the class teaching.

Coming back to the ACRL Framework, attempting to teach threshold concepts in two library sessions is ambitious. As ACRL expresses it, the Framework is intended to be taught over time because threshold concepts are metacognitive concepts.[15] In this view, assessment of a threshold concept needs to be done over time, as Megan Oakleaf states in her article "A Roadmap for Assessing Student Learning Using the New Framework for Information Literacy for Higher Education."[16] Consequently, it would make sense to revisit and continue exploring the taught threshold concepts in subsequent marketing courses. Linked to these issues is the question of to what extent the learned material and expected research behavior are sustainable. Students do not necessarily take skills from one course to the next. In other words, it might happen that students do very well on research and documenting their research in the co-designed class but do not perform research well or at all in other courses—either later in their academic career or during the same semester.[17]

Having taught the co-designed course for various semesters and seeing the importance of real-life learning experience for students, we think it worth considering how marketing professionals define and relate to information in their workplace. At the 2017 European Conference on Information Literacy, Bonnie Cheuk in her keynote, "Who Cares about Information Literacy in the Workplace?" took this perspective and illustrated what specific skills are needed in her profession.[18] She defined the term *workplace information literacy* for marketing professionals without referring to any definition such as the ACRL Framework. For librarians, instructors, and instructional designers in general, this approach might be very helpful in creating high-impact scenarios for students.

Notes

1. Sam Wineburg and Sarah McGrew, "Lateral Reading and the Nature of Expertise: Reading Less and Learning More When Evaluating Digital Information" (unpublished paper, Stanford Digital Repository, Stanford Libraries, July 28, 2018), 1, https://purl.stanford.edu/yk133ht8603.
2. Tom Kelly and Jonathan Littman, *The Ten Faces of Innovation* (New York: Currency/Doubleday, 2005).
3. Samantha Godbey and Xan Goodman, "Co-design: Integrating Information Literacy into Your Disciplinary Course" (AMICAL workshop, American University of Paris, March 31–April 1, 2017), https://www.amicalnet.org/events/co-design-integrating-information-literacy-into-your-disciplinary-course.

4. Association of College and Research Libraries, *Framework for Information Literacy for Higher Education* (Chicago: Association of College and Research Libraries, 2016), http://www.ala.org/acrl/standards/ilframework.
5. Melissa Bowles-Terry and Cassandra Kvenild, *Classroom Assessment Techniques for Librarians* (Chicago: Association of College and Research Libraries, 2015), 2–8.
6. Carol Collier Kuhlthau, "Students and the Information Search Process: Zones of Intervention for Librarians," in *Advances in Librarianship*, vol. 18, ed. Irene P. Godden (Bingley, UK: Emerald Group, 1994), 57–72, https://doi.org/10.1108/S0065-2830(1994)0000018004.
7. Alison J. Head and Michael B. Eisenberg, "Lessons Learned: How College Students Seek Information in the Digital Age," SSRN, December 1, 2009: 3, https://doi.org/10.2139/ssrn.2281478.
8. Michael Stöpel, "'How Do You Research?' The Non-use of Library Resources in Academic Research: A Case Study among Undergraduate Students at the American University of Paris" (MLIS thesis, American University of Paris, 2010), 65.
9. David R. Lankes, *Expect More* (North Charleston, SC: CreateSpace, 2016), 58.
10. Scott Bennett, "Putting Learning into Library Planning," *portal: Libraries and the Academy* 15, no. 2 (April 2015): 227, https://doi.org/10.1353/pla.2015.0014.
11. Rowan University Information Literacy Task Force, *Integrating Information Literacy into Rowan University Curriculum* (Glassboro, NJ: Rowan University, December 2002), 1–15.
12. Claire McGuinness, "Exploring Strategies for Integrated Information Literacy: From 'Academic Champions' to Institution-wide Change," *Communications in Information Literacy* 1, no. 1 (2007): 26–38, https://doi.org/10.15760/comminfolit.2007.1.1.5.
13. McGuinness, "Exploring Strategies," 34.
14. Bruce T. Sajdak, "Let the Faculty Do It: Responsibility and Collaboration in Developing an Information Literacy Program," *College and Research Libraries News* 73, no. 4 (April 2012): 196–99, https://doi.org/10.5860/crln.73.4.8740.
15. Association of College and Research Libraries, *Framework*, 8.
16. Megan Oakleaf, "A Roadmap for Assessing Student Learning Using the New Framework for Information Literacy for Higher Education," *Journal of Academic Librarianship* 40, no. 5 (September 2014): 512, https://doi.org/10.1016/j.acalib.2014.08.001.
17. Stöpel, "How Do You Research?" 45.
18. Bonnie Cheuk, "Who Cares about Information Literacy in the Workplace?" (keynote address, European Conference on Information Literacy [ECIL], Saint-Malo, France, September 18–21, 2017), 3.

Bibliography

Association of College and Research Libraries. *Framework for Information Literacy for Higher Education*. Chicago: Association of College and Research Libraries, 2016. http://www.ala.org/acrl/standards/ilframework.

Bennett, Scott. "Putting Learning into Library Planning." *portal: Libraries and the Academy* 15, no. 2 (April 2015): 215–31. https://doi.org/10.1353/pla.2015.0014.

Bowles-Terry, Melissa, and Cassandra Kvenild. *Classroom Assessment Techniques for Librarians.* Chicago: Association of College and Research Libraries, 2015.

Cheuk, Bonnie. "Who Cares about Information Literacy in the Workplace?" Keynote address, European Conference on Information Literacy (ECIL), Saint-Malo, France, September 18–21, 2017.

Collier Kuhlthau, Carol. "Students and the Information Search Process: Zones of Intervention for Librarians." In *Advances in Librarianship*, vol. 18. Edited by Irene P. Godden, 57–72. Bingley, UK: Emerald Group, 1994. https://doi.org/10.1108/S0065-2830(1994)0000018004.

Godbey, Samantha, and Xan Goodman. "Co-design: Integrating Information Literacy into Your Disciplinary Course." AMICAL workshop, American University of Paris, March 31–April 1, 2017. https://www.amicalnet.org/events/co-design-integrating-information-literacy-into-your-disciplinary-course.

Head, Alison J., and Michael B. Eisenberg. "Lessons Learned: How College Students Seek Information in the Digital Age." SSRN, December 1, 2009. https://doi.org/10.2139/ssrn.2281478.

Kelly, Tom, and Jonathan Littman. *The Ten Faces of Innovation: IDEO's Strategies for Beating the Devil's Advocate and Driving Creativity throughout Your Organization.* New York: Currency/Doubleday, 2005.

Lankes, David R. *Expect More: Demanding Better Libraries for Today's Complex World.* North Charleston, SC: CreateSpace, 2016.

McGuinness, Claire. "Exploring Strategies for Integrated Information Literacy: From 'Academic Champions' to Institution-wide Change." *Communications in Information Literacy* 1, no. 1 (2007): 26–38. https://doi.org/10.15760/comminfolit.2007.1.1.5.

Oakleaf, Megan. "A Roadmap for Assessing Student Learning Using the New Framework for Information Literacy for Higher Education." *Journal of Academic Librarianship* 40, no. 5 (September 2014): 510–14. https://doi.org/10.1016/j.acalib.2014.08.001.

Rowan University Information Literacy Task Force. *Integrating Information Literacy into Rowan University Curriculum.* Glassboro, NJ: Rowan University, December 2002.

Sajdak, Bruce T. "Let the Faculty Do It: Responsibility and Collaboration in Developing an Information Literacy Program." *College and Research Libraries News* 73, no. 4 (April 2012): 196–99. https://doi.org/10.5860/crln.73.4.8740.

Stöpel, Michael. "'How Do You Research?' The Non-use of Library Resources in Academic Research: A Case Study among Undergraduate Students at the American University of Paris." MLIS thesis, American University of Paris, 2010.

Wineburg, Sam, and Sarah McGrew. "Lateral Reading and the Nature of Expertise: Reading Less and Learning More When Evaluating Digital Information." Unpublished paper, Stanford Digital Repository, Stanford Libraries, July 28, 2018. https://purl.stanford.edu/yk133ht8603.

CASE STUDY 3

Integrating Information Literacy in a Communication Writing Course

Antonio Lopez, PhD

Chair and Associate Professor of Communications and Media Studies, John Cabot University, Rome, Italy

Livia Piotto

Reference and Instruction Coordinator, Frohring Library, John Cabot University, Rome, Italy

Elizabeth Macias-Gutiérrez, PhD

Lecturer in Communications, John Cabot University, Rome, Italy

Introduction

From fall 2017 to fall 2018, the Department of Communications at John Cabot University collaborated with Livia Piotto, Reference and Instruction Coordinator for the Frohring Library, to co-design and implement an information literacy strategy for a preexisting communications course, Writing across the Media (COM 221). In each semester, there were two sections with approximately twenty students each (totaling about eighty students overall for the entire academic year). The sections were taught by both Antonio Lopez and Elizabeth Macias-Gutiérrez. The sections were attended by a mix of freshmen and sophomores and a combination of resident degree seekers and visiting study-abroad students. John Cabot University is a four-year US-accredited undergraduate liberal arts college in Rome, Italy, that is approximately half study-abroad from the US and half resident degree seekers from over seventy-five different countries. This chapter reviews and discusses the results of this collaboration and also includes a reflection about how this collaboration can be improved.

Background

Writing across the Media (COM 221) is a core required course for communications majors at John Cabot University. The class was originally designed by Lopez to address the need for first- and second-year communications students to develop specific writing and research skills for a variety of different media (multimedia, audiovisual, podcasting, and strategic communications). In this writing-intensive course, students are exposed to writing techniques for different formats to help them gain insights into how each medium has different characteristics but also to help prepare them for upper-level courses. The course was designed to support the Department of Communications' philosophy of combining theory with media practice. It was also meant to help students prepare for careers in media and gain practical skills for the kinds of activities and projects they will likely have to engage in upon graduation. For example, the culminating assignment is to create a press kit, which is the most fundamental document that media organizations create, circulate, and read. Teaching students the ability to research, write, and create a press kit prepares them for practically any entry-level media job. From a theoretical point of view, by learning how to write for various media platforms, students learn about the affordances and constraints of different media. From a skill-based perspective, the course is meant to teach them basic research techniques, improve their writing, and hone their ability to design and execute strategic communication. The learning outcomes were initially designed as follows:

1. Learn legal and ethical principles of writing for the media.
2. Demonstrate an understanding of the history and role of writing for various media professions.
3. Write correctly and clearly in forms and styles appropriate for a variety of communications professions.

4. Apply tools and technologies appropriate for different communications professions.
5. Critically assess institutional and individual media practices.
6. Understand how to promote and share written works online.
7. Conceive, draft, edit, and finalize a basic script for visual and audio media.

In spring 2017, Lopez and Piotto attended the AMICAL-sponsored workshop aimed at co-designing learning outcomes for a pilot course in fall 2017.[1] They identified Writing across the Media as the ideal course to teach information literacy because it is required for all communications students and is a lower-level course that includes many assignments involving research and requiring an obvious information literacy component. The most important result after the workshop was the revision of the course learning outcomes, with the inclusion of two information literacy–specific outcomes to demonstrate a commitment to a deeper integration of information literacy within the course. The resulting learning outcomes were designed as follows:

1. Apply legal and ethical principles to writing for the media.
2. Critically assess institutional and individual media practices.
3. Distinguish the affordances and constraints of different media platforms as they relate to writing.
4. Write clearly in forms and styles appropriate for a variety of media formats.
5. Apply appropriate communication tools to media writing activities.
6. Identify, find, and verify authoritative information sources to develop strategic communication.
7. Apply research methods and strategies that are appropriate for communication tasks.

While we were trying to create more measurable outcomes, the clearest changes were made to outcomes five, six, and seven. Based on the co-design workshop, we incorporated specific language from the ACRL *Framework for Information Literacy for Higher Education* so that research methods and information literacy would be the primary focus. The language "appropriate communication tools" refers to the variety of information literacy tools that students should learn in order to improve their writing. In addition, and following the Framework, we stressed how the students should become information creators, and not merely information users, to apply "ways of thinking and practicing" to the discipline.[2]

Activity Design

As a result of the workshop in Paris, Lopez and Piotto collaborated to develop an implementation plan aimed at identifying in which ways the librarian was to contribute to the course and in which moment of the semester. Lopez and Piotto developed a number of information literacy activities that would be built into preexisting assignments and would be integrated into multiple sessions conducted by the librarian. The activities were designed with the six frames from the ACRL Framework in mind, and they were meant to be included in the library sessions. Initially, Lopez and Piotto thought of distributing the information literacy component of the course into two sessions, but the plan changed when the activities started to take shape. We ended up splitting information that was supposed to be delivered in one single session into separate sessions to make the delivered content more relevant to what the students were doing at different moments throughout the semester and to better respond to possible bottlenecks that the students could face. These changes came as a direct result of the participation in the workshop because we thought more in terms of the course timeline, and we tried to structure the course in a way that could help students scaffold skills, rather than just throwing all the information into one single library session. The decision to accommodate more information literacy instruction in separate sessions gave us the opportunity to include all six frames in some capacity.

Writing across the Media is structured in four different modules, each of which culminates in an assignment: news curation blog, public service announcement script, podcast script, and press kit. The course was not restructured in terms of major assignments, but we tied specific skills and activities suggested during the Paris workshop to each assignment. The idea of providing one information literacy session in each module was rejected, mostly to avoid repetition of concepts given that the activities we had developed would cover skills that the students could apply in more than one assignment. Table CS3.1 shows how each activity developed after the Paris workshop was incorporated into one or more assignments. The assignments were given in the order from left to right.

Table CS3.1

Matrix of information literacy activities according to assignment

Information literacy activity	**News Curation Blog**	**PSA Script**	**Podcast Script**	**Press Kit**
Examine coverage of controversial event	X			X
Book/film review	X		X	X
Compare and contrast sources	X	X		X
Research an organization (media)	X			X
Find suitable information	X	X		X
Research facts, statistics, data		X		X
Audience research		X		X
Trace scholar's career (interview)			X	

Before the Paris workshop, students were allowed to choose and develop their own topics for each assignment. Given that topic choice was one of the main bottlenecks in previous semesters, we decided that for more coherence and continuity during the semester, students would choose one topic from a predetermined list during the first assignment and then follow the same topic throughout the rest of the assignments. What follows is a more detailed breakdown of each assignment and activities.

Assignment 1: News Curation Blog

In assignment 1, students curate a media topic that is current in the news. A curator is a blogger who specializes in a specific topic or theme. A curator examines and evaluates a particular issue by assembling different materials and links to tell the story of the topic. Examples of topics that students could choose from included business of media, such as media consolidation and ownership issues; public media; surveillance and privacy; war and propaganda; fake news; representation, such as race, gender, LGBTQ, migrants, religion, or ethnic groups; net neutrality and the digital divide; media and the environment; and social movements and media.

Students were to write five blog posts related to the chosen topic (three posts about a controversial current event; a book, film, or media review; and an organizational profile). They were also required to set up a blog using WordPress or other preferred blogging platform. The research and information literacy activities included examining coverage of a controversial event, writing a book or film review, finding suitable information, comparing and contrasting sources, and researching an organization.

Assignment 2: Public Service Announcement Script

For assignment 2, students were required to write a thirty-second public service announcement (PSA) script and storyboard to promote a cause related to the news curation topic. The PSA was to be for an existing organization. The PSA assignment was required to have a unique title, log line (a one-sentence summary of the story), treatment (paragraph summary), script, storyboard, and two-page reflection paper. The research and information literacy activities included finding suitable information; comparing and contrasting sources; researching facts, statistics, and data; and researching the audience.

Assignment 3: Podcast Script

For assignment 3, students were asked to script a podcast based on the designated blog topic in which the student was host. The show was to be like a "radio magazine" with different sections and features with varied content. It was to have at least three different sections that included an interview with a scholar, a film or book review, and an editorial (a polemical statement). Students were asked to turn in a treatment (no more than four sentences) with log line, a five-to-seven-page script with appropriate technical language and format for audio scripts, and a two-page paper describing their process. Research and information literacy activities included researching for quality book or film reviews and researching scholars to trace their careers in order to prepare the script for a podcast interview.

Assignment 4: Press Kit

For the final project, students were required to create a mock press kit for an imaginary event tied to the blog topic. The event could be a film screening, book signing, concert, fundraiser, or something of their own invention that featured a celebrity. Students had to submit a properly formatted cover letter targeted to an editor or media outlet and appropriate section with a clearly stated goal to get some kind of press coverage; press release; bio or background information sheet highlighting relevant information for the targeted pitch letter (with footnotes to document information sources); other information (reviews, press clippings); and a two-page paper explaining their strategy and goals. Research and information literacy outcomes and activities were examining coverage of a controversial event; writing a book or film review; comparing and contrasting sources; researching an organization (media); finding suitable information; researching facts, statistics, and data; researching audience; and tracing a scholar's career (interview).

Information Literacy Component

The design of the library session lesson plans was entirely finalized by the librarian based on the specific activities that had been agreed on during the workshop. At the first stage, the Framework was used to decode how the course was initially developed and to identify possible bottlenecks where the students were expected to get stuck. After deciding the points in the semester when information literacy sessions could help with these bottlenecks, the librarian took a closer look at the

Framework and identified which frames should be prioritized in the individual sessions. Using backward design principles, specific learning outcomes were created, and the lesson plans were subsequently designed around those learning outcomes.

The original implementation plan for the fall 2017 pilot course included three information literacy sessions conducted by the librarian, each of which was developed with specific learning outcomes addressing one or more frames. We initially only scheduled two 75-minute-long sessions to cover the research component of the first two assignments. Then, as the semester was moving along, we decided to add a third, shorter session aimed at teaching the search strategy that would help students complete the tracing the scholar's career activity. All the information literacy sessions were created as independent and stand-alone sessions. Nevertheless, each session built on skills and knowledge acquired in the previous ones in an attempt to integrate separate concepts into an incremental progression.

The first library session, because students were expected to write a series of blog posts on various content, addressed three frames: Information Has Value, Authority Is Constructed and Contextual, and Searching as Strategic Exploration. Through a mix of lecturing and practical activities, the main topics covered during the session were the analysis of different types of biases, how they affect news production, and how to evaluate and use controversial news.[3] Initially, we decided to also include in this first session two other activities that the students would have reused, not only for the blog curation assignment but also for the podcast and the press kit: research for book or movie reviews and for media organization profiles. However, we noticed that trying to cover too much in a single class was not productive; in some cases the students needed more time for the single activities, and they needed more practical examples. Therefore, at the end of the pilot we decided to give more time to the review research and to the organization profile. In spring 2018, these two activities were expanded into two individual sessions. Although these sessions were shorter than the regular class period, separating these activities into individual sessions allowed more time for explaining the activities, providing more examples, and giving students time to practice.

A library session for the public service announcement script assignment was the only session that had been previously delivered as a one-shot session for a different course; the structure and content remained substantially the same, although a more precise alignment to the Framework was reached.[4] The frames supporting this lesson plan were Information Creation as a Process, Searching as Strategic Exploration, and Information Has Value. The active learning component in this second 75-minute-long session was very strong to avoid long lecturing moments. The students seemed to be more responsive to group discussions and individual work, whereas they seemed to appreciate less Think-Pair-Share type of activities. The last mini-session (forty to fifty minutes) was developed to introduce the students to the activity aimed at researching a scholar's career. This activity was designed as a way to engage the students in researching something unusual that could also be used as preliminary work for writing the script for their podcast assignment. Similarly to the other sessions, the mini-session outcomes complement many frames, but particularly they complement Scholarship as Conversation.

Discussion

Throughout the pilot semester, students experienced various challenges. Some of the activities we developed to clarify troublesome concepts instead became new bottlenecks for the students. For instance, although researching an organization seemed pretty straightforward as an activity, many felt uncomfortable writing organizational profiles without seeing a model first; students lacked the skills to summarize and were afraid to try something new. The film or book reviews tended to be superficial and descriptive and not analytical. As a result, further guidelines were developed to get students to probe deeper. When it came to researching facts and data, students needed a precise definition of data (i.e., types of evidence—quotes, statistics, etc.) and a better understanding of quality publications. For the tracing a scholar's career activity, students had difficulties when scholars didn't respond to interview requests. The solution was to curate interviews. Another challenge was to get students to understand news value and news hooks when writing their cover letters and preparing press kits. Moreover, library sessions can take time away from other instruction and workshop opportunities.

In terms of long-term lifelong learning skills, it was challenging to get students to develop the habit of always checking the source. As mentioned, when they were choosing a topic (even from a list), students had difficulty linking their passions and interests to a research topic. Finally, it is difficult to assess threshold concepts without long-term follow-up (i.e., Did the skills learned carry over to other classes and past the semester?).

Despite these challenges, already after just one semester there were numerous successes. Importantly, students learned to identify bias and develop PSA ideas from researching facts, and they produced interesting and compelling projects. Some significant strategies for success included limiting choice of topics (commit in first class through roundtable discussion); helping students find what they are passionate about; giving more detailed guidelines; repeating opportunities for practice throughout the semester and have students practice over and over again; choosing one topic across all the assignments to enable students to go deeper; and triangulating with three sources per post (from established news outlets).

Revision Process

Having seen the challenges and successes after the pilot course, Lopez, Macias-Gutiérrez, and Piotto decided to slightly revise the information literacy component added to the course. With the Framework foundations already in place, it was just a matter of adjusting the content of the library sessions and restructuring some of them in terms of length and point in the semester.

A first revision happened after the fall 2017 pilot course, and the result was the inclusion of two 75-minute sessions (the evaluation of news and biases, and the PSA research) and three shorter sessions focused on smaller and to-the-point assignments for the research for reviews, organizational profiles, and scholars' careers. A second revision was conducted before the fall 2018 course, once again to adjust the contents of the information literacy component of the course based on faculty-librarian post-session reflections, student reactions to the information literacy sessions, and the results of the librarian's continuous assessment of the library instruction component.[5] This revision process incorporated the students' perspectives through informal comments during and after the library sessions and in their end-of-semester course evaluations. The librarian's reflection on the observational assessment conducted after the long information literacy sessions provides some evidence for validating the students' engagement and their overall performance during the in-class activities.[6]

The second revision of the course brought a new restructuring of the sessions in terms of their length within the regular class period. As a result of faculty-librarian discussions, we included four long sessions (seventy-five minutes) with more active learning activities: evaluation of news and biases, book or movie review and media organization research, facts and statistics research for the PSA, and scholar's career research. This decision met the need to better integrate troublesome information literacy concepts without disrupting too much the regular flow of the course.

Following librarian-faculty discussions regarding student research performance, we have continued to develop strategies to address ongoing challenges and discover the potential behind these. To a certain extent, undergraduate students have an initial reticence to use library resources outside of the classroom, which, from our observations, could be attributed to some of the following scenarios: insufficient research exploration time outside the library session; minor difficulties in accessing the resources (particularly for study-abroad students off campus); limited value given to research; being intimidated by the research process; lack of patience when looking for specific content; and limited knowledge of useful resources.

Librarian-Faculty Joint Sessions

After the preparatory work done during the Paris workshop, we have settled on joint information literacy sessions that are led by the librarian with the support of the faculty. In a nutshell, the librarian-faculty joint sessions are a work in progress consisting of librarian seminars and workshops assisted by the professor and followed up by a research assignment that is usually initiated during the joint session. This research assignment, created as a result of the collaboration between the librarian and the professor, is constructed as a crucial activity toward the completion of each student's project. Each library session is thus divided into two parts: a training seminar session conducted by the librarian and a hands-on workshop where students work on the specific research assignment, while being assisted by the professor and the librarian. Such joint sessions require the professor to organize the class schedule in collaboration with the librarian in order to ensure that students come prepared to the library session with specific topics or other content to be used in the workshop.

The idea behind this dynamic emerged when contrasting the positive research outcome of students' PSA research to the improvement needed for the news curation research. The PSA research mainly consists of the creation of a fact sheet, which is a research document with information from varied sources to back up the content and claims implicit in the video script. One activity conducted by the librarian during the PSA library session involves an individual research exercise that prepares students to create this fact sheet. Students fill out the research handout with three or four types of evidence about issues to be addressed in the PSA video script. This handout is then collected by the librarian at the end of the session as part of the observational assessment.

Realizing how quickly and efficiently students filled out this handout during the joint workshop, the professor followed the same format for the creation of the fact sheet. Students are required to find specific content from at least five sources (in addition to those found for the librarian's handout) and categorize the sources according to the type of evidence and type of publication. This fact sheet is then submitted to the professor for written and oral feedback in the following class. A final version of the PSA fact sheet is later integrated with the final PSA submission. After these librarian-faculty joint workshops and fact sheet assignments, we have noticed more focused and varied research by students over the past few semesters. Students show more familiarity and dexterity when using resources such as Statista, Pew Research Center, ResearchGate, and LexisNexis. In addition, students have given feedback that this research experience has significantly inspired them in the storytelling and creation of the video scripts.

In contrast, there had not been a similar research handout or assignment for the news curation blog until fall 2018. Student research performance is assessed in the submission of their first blog post draft. In this submission for feedback, it was noticeable that students tend to rely on Google search, blogs, or even social media as their first tools of information (instead of using LexisNexis to target newspapers and news agencies such as Reuters or Associated Press). During the last semester, however, a strategy similar to the PSA research assignment was implemented. Students were required to submit a blog post draft that included hyperlinks to news articles found in LexisNexis. The librarian supported this news research by providing a media bias chart and a fact-checking website. From this submission, the professor was able to give more specific feedback on news quality and diversity of sources. Consequently, in the final submission, there was a noticeable improvement in news research and evaluation for most students. Once students were familiar with LexisNexis and realized how useful it is, they continued to use it to inform their PSA research as well as the press kit project. Some students also continued to use the media bias chart and fact-checking website for general reference throughout the course, even without the professor particularly requiring it. The fact that students reused sources and strategies taught in previous library sessions provides preliminary evidence that the distribution of the frames and their activities throughout the semester works and helps students build stronger research skills.

Another successful outcome of the joint sessions was perceived during the scholar research podcast session, which is one that students feel particularly intimidated by because they must contact and interview a scholar outside the university. Following the library instruction seminar, during which the librarian explained how research is a crucial aspect in the preparation of the materials needed to construct and structure an interview, the hands-on workshop allowed the professor and the librarian to support students in many different ways, from basic use of WorldCat Identities, ResearchGate, Academia.edu, and Google Scholar, to finding a scholar expert in a specific topic, to accessing the scholar's publications. In the following lecture, the follow-up consisted of students informing the professor about their scholar research progress and being given an assignment that provided the professor with the details and status of the scholar contacted. The outcome was positive. Aside from finding a scholar, many students showed interest in reading more about the work of the scholar before crafting the interview questions. In the reflection papers submitted with the podcast projects, students expressed satisfaction with having discussed a topic of interest with an expert in person or via e-mail, Skype, or phone. They also commented on how much credibility a scholar's input can bring to their podcast show.

A second collaborative aspect pertains to a minor reorganization of the library session calendar. The relationship between library sessions, assignments, and course schedule requires minor schedule adjustments to ensure that students attend the library session prepared to work on the specific research activity and follow up with an assignment accordingly. In addition, another modification was the anticipation and the expansion of the scholar research podcast session so that students had more in-class time to begin their research with the assistance of the professor and the librarian and could contact the chosen scholars with advance notice. As a result, an improvement in scholar response has been observed. Lastly, two library sessions, the book or movie review and the organizational profile blog post classes, were combined into one in order to allow an extra regular session with the professor and to offer students more time to write their blog post drafts after meeting with the librarian.

Finally, a third part of the collaboration was the creation of handouts with specific guidelines that connect the librarian's research sessions with the project requirements mentioned in the rubric. Faculty put together these handouts particularly for the review and organization profile content blog posts, where more critical and focused content needed to be developed. Students now tend to follow the guidelines, producing more critical reviews and organizational profiles.

We have been able to monitor improvements in the quality of research and an increasing interest and awareness of the possibilities of accessing relevant and interesting information beyond students' own smart devices.

From this joined dynamic, the following list provides general observations:

- We realized that these joint sessions can elevate the value that students give to research and allow them to better appreciate how central this step is toward the realization of the content and design of their projects.
- Students and faculty feel supported when they face a technical problem with the library resources and the librarian is present to resolve it. This helps students build research confidence.
- Both the librarian and faculty member can offer research direction as needed, offering research tips that allow students to move forward and build their own research map.
- The professor also has the opportunity to monitor student progress, answer questions, and inform the librarian of what research issues they need to target.
- The content that the librarian covers prompts numerous questions on how the assignment and project should be completed, and the professor is there to answer them.

What's Next for the Collaboration

The collaboration continues to develop as a work in progress through debriefing meetings between librarian and faculty, which serve as an opportunity to recap and continue discussing observations of student performance; students' preferences when interacting with software technology; how students can best take advantage of library resources; and trying out different scenarios in response. This creates a process of ongoing revision, and the activities continue to be updated to better respond to the course needs. Furthermore, some immediate objectives for the librarian-faculty collaboration that emerged from the joint session are to:

- finalize a news curation research assignment based on specific knowledge practices and dispositions from the Framework to follow up the library session;
- build a more structured research exercise for the review and organizational profile sessions with specific learning outcomes informed by the Framework;
- continue to inform each other's sessions and share material while avoiding some overlap of information;
- collect more material in terms of examples to further develop a "Show, Don't Tell" mentality;
- collect more press kit samples that cover various types of events;
- follow up on scholarly content found by students but accessed only for a fee, with a specific focus on open access content that could substitute for the for-a-fee content;
- address study-abroad students' off-campus access;[7] and
- assist students when they are researching content in a foreign language.

The aspect in need of further development is clearly the assessment of the threshold concepts identified within the six frames. Now that information literacy has become an official part of the course with the integration of dedicated course learning outcomes, we need to reach a deeper level of collaboration in terms of assessment. Though each information literacy session has its own learning outcomes, we need to expand the assessment of the library instruction activities by implementing a different type of assessment, beyond the mere classroom assessment techniques already in place;[8] and especially we need to better integrate the information literacy assessment into the main course activities and not limit its scope to the in-class activities developed for the library session. The biggest challenge remains the difficulty of assessing threshold concepts in the long term. Ideally we could develop a course assessment plan aiming to collect formative (from the information literacy sessions) and summative (from the course activities) assessment data to close the loop and verify whether the students have achieved the overall course outcomes.

Overall, this experience has not only been valuable for the librarian and the students, but it has also offered a greater perspective for faculty in terms of students' challenges and needs. Using the Framework allowed the professors to define the broader concepts that were the foundation for their specific assignments and to identify how the librarian can bring her expertise to collaborate with faculty to help students reach this goal. However, the more this work progresses, the more we want to test different strategies and improve current models. As we said multiple times, this collaborative project was born as a work in progress, and it remains as such through continuous assessment of the work done and the outcomes reached, reflection on student performance, and revision of the information literacy activities.

Notes

1. Samantha Godbey and Xan Goodman, "Co-design: Integrating Information Literacy into Your Disciplinary Course" (AMICAL workshop, American University of Paris, March 31–April 1, 2017), https://www.amicalnet.org/events/co-design-integrating-information-literacy-into-your-disciplinary-course.
2. Association of College and Research Libraries, *Framework for Information Literacy for Higher Education* (Chicago: Association of College and Research Libraries, 2016), http://www.ala.org/acrl/standards/ilframework.
3. See the lesson plan for the revised session, "Evaluating News through the Exploration of Bias," in this book.
4. See the full lesson plan, "What's behind That? Facts and Statistics Supporting Public Service Announcements," in this book. This version of the lesson plan was revised after the fall 2017 pilot and delivered as part of the course in spring and fall 2018.
5. Megan Oakleaf, "The Information Literacy Instruction Assessment Cycle: A Guide for Increasing Student Learning and Improving Librarian Instructional Skills," *Journal of Documentation* 65, no. 4 (2009): 539–60, https://doi.org/10.1108/00220410910970249.
6. Details about the observational assessment can be found in the lesson plans "Evaluating News through the Exploration of Bias" and "What's behind That? Facts and Statistics Supporting Public Service Announcements."
7. Study-abroad students, not having a JCU email address to authenticate themselves on the library resources, need special instructions for remote access when doing research using subscriptions resources off campus.
8. Classroom assessment techniques (CATs) have already been used in the context of this course's library sessions based on examples taken from the classic book by Thomas A. Angelo and K. Patricia Cross, *Classroom Assessment Techniques*, 2nd ed. (San Francisco: Jossey-Bass, 1993) and from Melissa Bowles-Terry and Cassandra Kvenild, *Classroom Assessment Techniques for Librarians* (Chicago: Association of College and Research Libraries, 2015).

Bibliography

Angelo, Thomas A., and K. Patricia Cross. *Classroom Assessment Techniques: A Handbook for College Teachers*, 2nd ed. San Francisco: Jossey-Bass Publishers, 1993.

Association of College and Research Libraries. *Framework for Information Literacy for Higher Education*. Chicago: Association of College and Research Libraries, 2016. http://www.ala.org/acrl/standards/ilframework.

Bowles-Terry, Melissa, and Cassandra Kvenild. *Classroom Assessment Techniques for Librarians*. Chicago: Association of College and Research Libraries, 2015.

Godbey, Samantha, and Xan Goodman. "Co-design: Integrating Information Literacy into Your Disciplinary Course." AMICAL workshop, American University of Paris, March 31–April 1, 2017. https://www.amicalnet.org/events/co-design-integrating-information-literacy-into-your-disciplinary-course.

Oakleaf, Megan. "The Information Literacy Instruction Assessment Cycle: A Guide for Increasing Student Learning and Improving Librarian Instructional Skills." *Journal of Documentation* 65, no. 4 (2009): 539–60. https://doi.org/10.1108/00220410910970249.

CASE STUDY 4

Teaching Information Literacy in Kuwait

Achievements, Challenges, and Future Recommendations

Stavros P. Hadjisolomou, PhD

Department of Social and Behavioral Sciences, First Year Experience Program, College of Arts and Sciences, American University of Kuwait, Safat, Kuwait

Background: Why Is a Liberal Arts Education Important for Teaching Information Literacy?

While research on the topic of information literacy (IL) in Kuwait is limited, studies have found students and professionals in this region to be ill-equipped for searching and using information.[1] Due to a general lack of educational initiatives in the past, the concept of IL is virtually unknown to the broader population in Kuwait. For example, when incoming students at the American University of Kuwait (AUK) were prompted during the first class of an introductory first year experience course to define *information literacy*, none have been able to demonstrate an understanding of the term. Similarly, when students are presented with common forms of plagiarism later in the semester, some have difficulty accepting some examples as violations of academic integrity. Even worse, a few individuals did not understand why "paying someone, or paying a service, for a paper and turning it in as your own work" is considered dishonest.[2] Through personal communication with college students from different universities and colleges in Kuwait, I learned that such behaviors are usually cultivated during secondary education. It is not uncommon, for example, for hired tutors or teachers to be tasked with producing essays for their clients' school assignments.

As a direct result of such demand, there exists a market in Kuwait where students can buy services such as a customized essay written for an English course, an art piece for a graphic design course, or a technical project for an engineering course. Sadly, some students do not believe that using such services creates a problem of academic dishonesty because they are paying to receive help with their assignments. In other words, a financial transaction is thought to legitimize the service, and thus there is no problem in receiving credit for someone else's work if a student paid for it in the first place. We utilize such anecdotes as class discussion prompts to examine how ethical behavior is one of the essential elements of learning and also to help develop an appreciation for the value in creating content as information. These discussions demonstrate the significance of a broad liberal arts education in developing the student holistically within the domains of self, such as ethical, intellectual, and vocational.

While the problem described here is a serious one and requires further attention, a more significant problem can be seen in low academic performance due to a lack of sufficient mastery of IL skills. Even in cases when students understand the ethical and professional problems of plagiarism, they may score low in IL competencies, resulting in poor academic performance when completing university-level assignments. In the next sections, I provide background information on the learning outcomes, mission, and vision statements of the First Year Experience program and the library at AUK. These will help situate the reader on how the collaborative efforts of the FYE-Library team set out to meet our students' and faculty's needs in promoting IL skills in a small liberal arts university in Kuwait.

Description of Institution and Student Demographics

AUK is an independent, private, equal opportunity, and coeducational four-year liberal arts institution. Currently, there are approximately 2,500 to 3,000 undergraduate students enrolled, of whom 58 percent are female and 42 percent male. Sixty-four percent of the students are Kuwaiti nationals, 27 percent are Arabs from either the Gulf Cooperation Council (GCC) or non-GCC Arab countries, and the remaining 9 percent are from other countries.[3]

Description of First Year Experience and Library Co-design Team

Program

During the fall 2017 semester, the AUK Library and the First Year Experience program collaborated on co-designing a semester-long project for a first-year, two-credit academic course (UNIV 100: Essentials of Learning). A two-person team consisting of a library staff member, Zainab Al-Attabi, and assistant professor of psychology Dr. Stavros Hadjisolomou presented in-class workshops with the aim of helping incoming students develop their IL skills. This initiative was supplementary to an IL workshop provided by the library. The collaboration also served to extend the role of the library within AUK.

Mission Statements

The following statements were retrieved from the AUK website:

- AUK Library Mission: "The AUK Library supports research, teaching and learning needs of the AUK community through information resources, expertise, and innovative services."[4]
- IL strategic goal: "To expand and strengthen the library's teaching role and continue to provide an information literacy program that enhances critical thinking, academic success, and lifelong learning."[5]
- FYE program mission: "The First Year Experience strives to integrate all first-year students into the university's liberal arts environment by empowering them with essential academic, personal and social skills. Students learn through holistic and experiential methods that encourage self-assessment and reflection. Ultimately, students in the FYE program are encouraged to become empathetic leaders and active agents of change within their communities."[6]

- FYE program vision: "The FYE program hopes to add more campus-wide programs as well as work in partnership with other departments and campus organizations. We aim to develop a more community-based opportunities for students to apply interdisciplinary course concepts. By offering more professional development opportunities in the future, we aspire to inspire faculty and staff to promote learning campus-wide."[7]

Collaboration Goals

Students' Library Instruction Experience during High School

Students in Kuwait have had extremely diverse academic experiences upon entering university. The main factor underlying the differences in academic histories is the diversity of secondary education institutions in Kuwait. For example, high schools differ in type (public or private) and class size (from twenty students up to more than fifty per class). However, the main differences can be seen in the language of instruction (monolingual or bilingual—usually Arabic and English) and the country model of the school, if not a public school (American, British, Indian, Pakistani, Armenian, Philippine, French, etc.). The breadth of curricula taught also varies widely.

Due to such differences in schooling, it is rare for incoming AUK students to share common academic experiences involving library instruction or knowledge of using library resources to complete academic assignments. When asked to share their previous experiences of using the library resources, AUK students offered answers ranging from passive knowledge of the library's function to high levels of active involvement in utilizing said resources. Only a small subset of incoming students reported having participated in library workshops hosted at local universities as part of high school visits. On the other hand, the majority stated they used the library premises solely to complete homework assignments on available desktop computers and did not engage with any library staff nor employ any other available library resources.

Due to these reasons, many students lack awareness of basic IL skills and strategies. Thus, they are not capable of performing research tasks involving finding, citing, and analyzing appropriate sources for assignments at university-level standards. Similar to other students of their generation, many AUK students felt overwhelmed and confused about their assigned tasks and ultimately delayed in starting and finalizing their work.[8] Many of these students did not know how to use tools and resources other than Google or Wikipedia due to using the same sites to prepare identical assignments during their high school years with variable levels of success.

Negative Effects of Low Information Literacy Competencies on Academic Assignments and Current Interventions

The behavioral repertoire described above does not include basic IL strategies, resulting in low grades and, in turn, a decrease in students' self-esteem and academic self-efficacy. The FYE-Library co-design team speculates that these factors can have further harmful effects on students' academic performance and quite possibly on career tasks beyond the university. On a similar note, AUK faculty have anecdotally expressed concerns about student performance in IL skills required for initiating and completing academic writing assignments. In their experience, some students are often ill-equipped to perform scholarly research as a requirement of their academic assignments due to a lack of general understanding of what IL skills are and how to best utilize them. If student and faculty perceptions of students' IL skills levels are accurate, then conceivably students may be neither equipped with basic research skills nor capable of meeting the minimum standards expected at the university level.

To help students develop such skills, the AUK library has been collaborating with the First Year Experience program in providing one-shot IL workshops as part of the requirements for a first-year UNIV 100 class assignment. During this workshop, students receive instruction on how to use tools and resources to complete their academic assignments. While all incoming students must complete and pass an assignment to receive credit for this one-shot workshop, a general lack of complementary types of assessment of IL skills has left the following questions unanswered: What do our students learn during this one-shot workshop? Is this learning outcome sufficient to help them succeed in reaching their current and future academic goals?

The FYE-Library co-design team focused on these two questions to redesign the UNIV 100 course with the purpose of collecting data and assessing our students' IL skills. In addition to the one-shot IL workshop, the team held two additional in-class instructional seminars to teach students strategic searching skills. We incorporated a semester-long project on social issues in Kuwait as a platform to practice and improve the specific strategic searching skills learned. For assessment purposes, we measured student IL skill levels before the course to determine the incoming baseline levels as well as post–course completion levels to identify performance gains. Lastly, we asked students to report on their subjective experience to see if their perceptions matched their measurable IL skills. The following sections describe the design and implementation steps, as well as challenges the team faced and positive outcomes as part of the process.

Redesigning UNIV 100

The Co-design Workshop at American University of Paris

Before the workshop "Co-design: Integrating Information Literacy into Your Disciplinary Course" at the American University of Paris,[9] the FYE-Library team had planned to create a project to promote IL skills and higher-order thinking skills to educate students about fake news and the issues of misinformation. However, as part of the workshop exercises, the team focused on identifying the importance of using the current class learning outcomes instead (see "Summary of Project Assignment and Learning Outcomes" section below). This was an essential step in clarifying the purpose of redesigning the course, and in this way, the workshop enabled both horizontal and vertical alignment of the UNIV 100 course outcomes with programmatic ones set by the FYE program, the library, and the university. As a direct outcome of the workshop, the team had a clear idea of how to characterize learning outcomes accurately, how to create appropriate assignments that would help students learn, and how to create assessments to measure how much students learned.

Brainstorming Sessions

The basics of the collaboration plan were discussed and designed before the fall 2017 semester. During several one-hour-long meetings that took place between May and July 2017, the FYE-Library team discussed possible ideas about the main objectives, how to align the task assignments to course learning outcomes, the type of information we would need to assess students' incoming IL skills properly, and, lastly, how to interpret existing data to contribute to our understanding of the students' strengths and weaknesses.

Choosing a Frame and Appropriate Types of Assessment: Challenges and Solutions

One of the significant challenges the team faced in redesigning the course was deciding on a rationale in choosing a specific frame to focus on from the *ACRL Framework for Information Literacy for Higher Education* and, in turn, designing a suitable project for the class.[10] The task of jointly examining all possible frames before ultimately choosing one of them caused a delay in setting the foundations for the project. In addition to this delay, we also encountered difficulties in identifying and selecting appropriate assessment tools to measure the IL competencies of our students because the Framework was recently published at the time.

The team tackled these challenges by sharing and discussing common experiences in teaching first-year students, both in the UNIV 100 classroom and also during library workshops. We reflected on the most frequent problems students face when completing tasks for their assignments. We opted to focus on identifying existing solutions to these problems because any new method created by our team would require testing for reliability and validity. Even though such tests would be essential, it would not be possible to fit them in the specific project time frame. Therefore, we decided to adopt any well-established tools to help us meet our objectives. For this purpose, the team contacted fellow librarians from a variety of institutions who shared several assessment tool options to explore.

After taking into consideration the opinion of AUK faculty with regard to low student competency in research skills, the team decided to focus on the frame Searching as Strategic Exploration. We utilized the following methods to assess our students' aptitude in this domain at the time of admission and at the end of our course:

- incorporation of the Threshold Achievement Test for Information Literacy (TATIL), a brand-new tool at the time;[11]
- use of student journals to measure proficiency in the following skills: number of strategies, use of search strategies, student explanation of strategy choices, reflective description of strengths and weaknesses of strategy choices, and revision of approach if students were to repeat the same project; and
- assessment of individual student presentations on a social issue in Kuwait.

Another noteworthy obstacle we faced was the nonoverlapping annual summer leave, during which the team could not meet for a month and a half, resulting in a halt of our operations in setting up the course. While the project's start date was not delayed, we feel that the team would have been better off by having more regular meetings during the month before the start of the project for more effective and efficient coordination and ability to focus.

Summary of Project Assignment and Learning Outcomes

The team decided to use an existing UNIV 100 project that tasked students with identifying and presenting a social issue in Kuwait with the objective of raising awareness and promoting in-class discussion. Students were to choose a topic, develop key search terms, and use the search tool to locate information on the social issue of their choice. They also had to journal their search processes, including key terms, strategies, tools used, and resources and results at each step. Finally, they had to note how they evaluated their resources and what information was extracted.

The learning outcomes were as follows:

- Demonstrate efficiency in planning, conducting, evaluating, and revising searches to achieve relevant results.
- Demonstrate an understanding of comparing and contrasting a range of search tools.

Students were tasked with practicing using strategic searching skills to identify appropriate sources on social issues. There are not many studies concerning social issues in Kuwait, and thus the task of finding relevant sources was challenging to first-year students. From a pedagogical perspective, a scarcity of sources can be regarded as problematic and thus could devalue the project's strategic searching objective. However, when the team discussed in class the general lack of studies in the region, students expressed their enthusiasm for and increased interest in the project since it became a challenging puzzle for them to solve. We feel this was an essential factor in improving student engagement in the project and served as a motivational factor in completing required tasks for the project.

The Librarian's Role in Designing Instruction around the Framework

The librarian used the learning outcomes of the project to design two in-class seminars for instructional purposes. The first seminar was primarily a visual presentation that introduced the library's databases, references, and other types of resources, as well as how to use them. Students were asked to practice using these tools at home as part of their assignment. During the second seminar, the librarian discussed the strengths and weaknesses of each of the strategies used by students and provided constructive feedback to help improve follow-up searches.

Implementation of the Project

In-Class Instruction Provided by the Library

We started the semester by having students complete the TATIL. Students then participated in a one-shot workshop provided by the library. Also, the librarian presented the two in-class seminars discussed above on how to use the available library databases to find and browse relevant abstracts and to narrow down sources to the most pertinent ones. During the first in-class seminar, students were put into groups and encouraged to discuss tasks such as identifying relevant keywords for their search. Later, students were also tasked with carrying out searches at home using these specific keywords while documenting the results. During the second session, students brought back their search results and received direct feedback from the instructional librarian. This step was essential in ensuring that all students had experienced and practiced the method of searching with variable rates of success as a learning phase, which served as a discussion point to help improve their strategies before they started to complete the project on their own. Lastly, students were tasked with completing the same TATIL test at the end of the semester so that the team could measure any performance gains as a result of the project.

Collaborative Dynamic between the Librarian and Faculty Partner

One of the significant obstacles to implementing the team's plan for the project was the observed low levels of class engagement during the first in-class librarian workshop. According to students' self-reports, the perception of the librarian's authority in the class was different from that of the primary instructor. Students exhibited lower levels of class etiquette and civility when the librarian was presenting, as seen in frequently attempted smartphone usage, chatting between students, and the general lack of active involvement. The faculty partner supported the librarian instructor by explaining to students how they would benefit from this collaboration by cultivating a transferable skill, essential for research at the college level and beyond. Students were generally receptive to the idea that their performance in future academic assignments would increase as a direct result of the project. Active involvement and motivation levels increased noticeably by the second instructional seminar; there was a lively discussion of how each student approached the task, what their results were, and how they revised keywords to improve their findings. Students were eager to share and receive tips on which strategies worked best. Overall, they were actively listening to the librarian and engaged in collaborative work to improve their follow-up searches.

Pre- and Post-assessments

As stated above, for assessment we employed the Threshold Achievement Test for Information Literacy (TATIL). The tool consists of multiple-choice questions and measures IL competency directly. There are different versions of the TATIL tool, each aimed to measure competency on a specific ACRL frame. For the purposes of our assessment, we used the test for Strategic Searching, which required students to answer questions on "planning, evaluating and revising searches during strategic exploration."[12] It is important to note that the TATIL is a commercial tool. Each institution interested in administering the TATIL will have to buy tests for the number of students to be assessed. In our case, we paid five dollars for each test we administered through funds provided by the American University of Kuwait to the library.

The assessment took place at two different periods, during the first week of the semester and one month before finals. The duration of the test session was fifty minutes. However, students were allowed to leave the room once they completed the questionnaire. Our team, with the assistance of IT personnel, handled the administration of the test. The TATIL tool collected all data from students' tests and generated reports of results. The primary aim of our assessment was formative; we intended to evaluate any weak spots of our IL workshops to revise and improve our teaching efficiency. Once student IL performance meets or exceeds adequate learning levels, our assessment will serve a summative role to provide evidence of impact on relevant AUK stakeholders in other departments who consider adopting this program.

Student Project Evaluation

The faculty-librarian team was responsible for grading and evaluating all student projects toward the end of the semester. Each project received a report with comments from the instructors as well as a letter grade based on perceived quality. We duplicated each report and gave one copy to the students, and another was stored as data to be analyzed.

Interestingly, when compared to other sections that had only the one-shot workshop without additional in-class instruction and projects, the students in our co-designed section showed marginally significant improvements in their knowledge and performance of IL skills, while the control group remained at the same pre-workshop levels. These improvements in IL skills are potential evidence of the direct benefit of the additional in-class workshops and thus the co-design collaboration in general. Additional semesters and studies with a larger sample size are required to determine if these results would hold and be generalized across the population.

Insights from Experience

Challenges

One of the design and implementation challenges we faced throughout the semester was the limitation of having to maintain the uniformity of all UNIV

100 sections, including the co-designed one, to prevent differences in learning outcomes, bias, and unfairness. Based on this experience, we advise interested individuals without prior experience in co-designing a course to start with classes where only a few sections are offered each semester, or better yet only one, to test their pilot design and implementation.

Students' proficiency in the English language can be a significant challenge in examining the relationship between the co-design project and its effects on IL skill performance. Our findings indicated a high correlation between these two variables, with students who scored lower on English proficiency tests (data provided by the institutional research office of AUK) also scoring lower in IL skills in both the TATIL pre- and posttests. The main point of this finding is that students will not be able to solve a problem correctly if they do not understand what the question means or what it is asking them to do. We advise colleagues from fellow international American universities to measure English proficiency as an additional variable in their designed studies. Additionally, if possible, groups can be matched based on this factor and other demographics that may help explain differences in IL skills, such as socioeconomic status, age, gender, and so on.

Time availability of both faculty and librarian members was another major issue we had to work with on this project. If we were to redo the project, a semester when the teaching load is minimal would be chosen so as to dedicate more time to tasks involving the IL in-class instruction. Nevertheless, the team made sure to allocate sufficient time to all necessary procedures.

Successes

When prompted, all students reported a desire to improve their research skills at the time. Thus, we were able to achieve a buy-in mentality before starting the project, which was important in terms of setting expectations of a direct self-benefit as an outcome of the project that resulted in high levels of student engagement with the class and tasks at hand. Overall, we received self-reports that students believed they had learned from the workshop and that their academic self-efficacy increased because they had achieved success in completing challenging tasks. When we also measured their IL skills directly, we found an agreement between the self-assessment and the direct skill assessment results.

An important key factor in the project's success is that collaboration does not need to be just between the two FYE-Library team members, but others can be recruited, given their shared interest in teaching IL skills. For example, when we explained the project and especially the significance of our learning outcomes, other FYE colleagues opted to help by having their students participate in our testing. From the library's end, Ms. Zainab recruited additional staff members to help with data collection. Furthermore, we talked ahead of time to IT staff about helping us set up the computers for our testing, and also to institutional research about helping us by providing demographic and academic data for the incoming students, necessary for our analysis.

By recruiting additional members of our university, we helped spread the word about the project so that we could find interested parties who could be part of the process. Some of these faculty members who believed our co-designed project was necessary helped by talking to their departments about adopting our plan in their classes. Now that the project has ended, we could present our results to such interested parties to get them involved and help continue the project in further disciplines. However, one of the significant obstacles is the lack of a sufficient number of instructional librarians who can help sustain this project; the existing library staff is often overwhelmed with current tasks, which makes it challenging to allocate further time for projects such as this one here.

Conclusions

Overall, we believe this project was a success and that we need to have more of these types of workshops in the future. Ideally, other disciplines can adopt the general idea of the seminar and incorporate it into their classrooms as a measure to improve students' skills that are currently lacking. We feel that including the same type of project in a different class type would be redundant because the skills are transferable. Instead, since there are several frames, it would make more sense to explore other skills that are necessary for producing strong evidence-based academic work by our students.

Notes

1. Sultan M. Al-Daihani and Sajjad ur Rehman, "A Study of the Information Literacy Capabilities of the Kuwaiti Police Officers," *Electronic Library* 25, no. 5 (2007): 613–26;

Nujoud Al-Muomen, Anne Morris, and Sally Maynard, "Modelling Information-Seeking Behaviour of Graduate Students at Kuwait University," *Journal of Documentation* 68, no. 4 (2012): 430–59; Abdus Sattar Chaudhry and Sarah Al-Mahmud, "Information Literacy at Work: A Study on Information Management Behaviour of Kuwaiti Engineers," *Electronic Library* 33, no. 4 (2015): 760–72; Teresa M. Lesher, "Information Literacy Instruction for Kuwaiti Students and the Role of Cultural Relevance" (doctoral dissertation, Loughborough University, 2002), https://dspace.lboro.ac.uk/2134/6804; Sajjad ur Rehman and Sumayyah Alfaresi, "Information Literacy Skills among Female Students in Kuwaiti High Schools," *Library Review* 58, no. 8 (2009): 607–16.

2. Joseph B. Cuseo et al., *Thriving in College and Beyond* (Dubuque, IA: Kendall Hunt, 2016), 159.
3. American University of Kuwait, "University Culture," http://www.auk.edu.kw/about-auk/the-university.
4. American University of Kuwait, "Mission," Overview, Library, https://www.auk.edu.kw/academics/library/about-us/overview.
5. American University of Kuwait, "Strategic Goals," Overview, Library, https://www.auk.edu.kw/academics/library/about-us/overview.
6. American University of Kuwait, "First Year Experience (FYE)," Academic Catalog 2017–2018, http://www.auk.edu.kw/pr/catalog/2018/fye.html.
7. American University of Kuwait, "First Year Experience."
8 Alison Head, "Project Information Literacy: What Can Be Learned about the Information-Seeking Behavior of Today's College Students?" in *Imagine, Innovate, Inspire: The Proceedings of the ACRL 2013 Conference*, ed. Dawn M. Mueller (Chicago: Association of College and Research Libraries, 2013), 417–82; Craig Gibson and Trudi E. Jacobson, "Informing and Extending the Draft ACRL Information Literacy Framework for Higher Education: An Overview and Avenues for Research," guest editorial, *College and Research Libraries* 75, no. 3 (2014): 250–54, https://doi.org/10.5860/0750250.
9. Samantha Godbey and Xan Goodman, "Co-design: Integrating Information Literacy into Your Disciplinary Course" (AMICAL workshop, American University of Paris, March 31–April 1, 2017), https://www.amicalnet.org/events/co-design-integrating-information-literacy-into-your-disciplinary-course.
10. Association of College and Research Libraries, *Framework for Information Literacy for Higher Education* (Chicago: Association of College and Research Libraries, 2016).
11. Threshold Achievement home page, https://thresholdachievement.com/.
12. Threshold Achievement, "Module 2: Strategic Searching," http://thresholdachievement.com/the-test/module-information?module=2.

Bibliography

Al-Daihani, Sultan M., and Sajjad ur Rehman. "A Study of the Information Literacy Capabilities of the Kuwaiti Police Officers." *Electronic Library* 25, no. 5 (2007): 613–26.

Al-Muomen, Nujoud, Anne Morris, and Sally Maynard. "Modelling Information-Seeking Behaviour of Graduate Students at Kuwait University." *Journal of Documentation* 68, no. 4 (2012): 430–59.

American University of Kuwait. "First Year Experience (FYE)." Academic Catalog 2017–2018. http://www.auk.edu.kw/pr/catalog/2018/fye.html.

———. "Mission." Overview, Library. https://www.auk.edu.kw/academics/library/about-us/overview.

———. "Strategic Goals." Overview, Library. https://www.auk.edu.kw/academics/library/about-us/overview.

———. "University Culture." http://www.auk.edu.kw/about-auk/the-university.

Association of College and Research Libraries. *Framework for Information Literacy for Higher Education.* Chicago: Association of College and Research Libraries, 2016.

Chaudhry, Abdus Sattar, and Sarah Al-Mahmud. "Information Literacy at Work: A Study on Information Management Behaviour of Kuwaiti Engineers." *Electronic Library* 33, no. 4 (2015): 760–72.

Cuseo, Joseph B., Aaron Thompson, Michele Campagna, and Viki S. Fecas. *Thriving in College and Beyond: Research-Based Strategies for Academic Success and Personal Development.* Dubuque, IA: Kendall Hunt, 2016.

Gibson, Craig, and Trudi E. Jacobson. "Informing and Extending the Draft ACRL Information Literacy Framework for Higher Education: An Overview and Avenues for Research." Guest editorial. *College and Research Libraries* 75, no. 3 (2014): 250–54. https://doi.org/10.5860/0750250.

Godbey, Samantha, and Xan Goodman. "Co-design: Integrating Information Literacy into Your Disciplinary Course." AMICAL workshop, American University of Paris, March 31–April 1, 2017. https://www.amicalnet.org/events/co-design-integrating-information-literacy-into-your-disciplinary-course.

Head, Alison. "Project Information Literacy: What Can Be Learned about the Information-Seeking Behavior of Today's College Students?" In *Imagine, Innovate, Inspire: The Proceedings of the ACRL 2013 Conference.* Edited by Dawn M. Mueller, 417–82. Chicago: Association of College and Research Libraries, 2013.

Lesher, Teresa M. "Information Literacy Instruction for Kuwaiti Students and the Role of Cultural Relevance." Doctoral dissertation, Loughborough University, 2002. https://dspace.lboro.ac.uk/2134/6804.

Threshold Achievement home page. https://thresholdachievement.com/.

Threshold Achievement. "Module 2: Strategic Searching." http://thresholdachievement.com/the-test/module-information?module=2.

ur Rehman, Sajjad, and Sumayyah Alfaresi. "Information Literacy Skills among Female Students in Kuwaiti High Schools." *Library Review* 58, no. 8 (2009): 607–16.

CASE STUDY 5

Amalia y Yo

A Case Study Using the ACRL Framework in the Specific Context of the FirstBridge Information Literacy Program at the American University of Paris

Jorge F. Sosa

University Librarian, American University of Paris, France

In this chapter I try to explain, through the example of one specific student and her trajectory at our university, how one librarian has tried to apply the ACRL *Framework for Information Literacy for Higher Education* in the context of the first-year information literacy program at the American University of Paris (AUP).[1] I explain AUP's FirstBridge program and its lifelong learning objectives, structure, and dynamics, as well as how I taught one FirstBridge session when the subjects were robotics and arts. I also present the challenges faced by one student and the librarian in dealing with Scholarship as Conversation and Information Creation as a Process. The author's question has been regarding the possibilities of integrating the new Framework in the context of our liberal arts institution. Can the ACRL Framework be taught at this level and for the disciplines of this specific FirstBridge?

AUP's "Fit" Student

It is important for every campus to define the type of student they want to recruit, and a few years ago at AUP, the campus started a reflection on this topic. AUP came up with the notion of the Global Explorer, a notion that reflects the profile of our very diverse student body. AUP has more than 100 student nationalities, and our students are mostly nomadic; they feel at home in just about any place on the globe. The majority come from families with parents from different nationalities and who have lived in multiple countries and come from very different cultures. Our students do not seem to have the intention of settling in one geographical point and building their lives in that spot; they rather foresee moving from one country to another and from one job to the next one. This notion of the Global Explorer has brought coherence in the type of services the campus provides, as well as in the development of academic services and pedagogical initiatives at AUP. We can easily take our Global Explorers to places to be explored in a complex and dynamic city like Paris. I will show later in this chapter how this has had an impact on the teaching of information literacy.

Information Literacy at AUP

In the spring of 2017, one of AUP`s film professors and I participated actively at the AMICAL Consortium's "Co-design: Integrating Information Literacy into Your Disciplinary Course" workshop,[2] where we became more familiar with the new ACRL *Framework for Information Literacy for Higher Education* and how to work better to incorporate the Framework into the course Sex, Gender and Cinema. The main goal of the workshop was to co-design the course activities together for the following fall. Both of us believe that we made some very interesting progress in terms of co-designing the class structure and the reflective seminars with the course, in addition to having a better understanding of the ACRL Framework. Personally, I felt a sense of urgency to start working with the Framework as well as to renew my pedagogy. In the fall of 2017, when the idea of this book came up, both of us were enthusiastic about the opportunity to write about our experience, but in the end other scholarly and professional projects did not allow the film professor to pursue our idea. I found myself without a chapter for this book until one morning a simple Facebook Messenger message arrived on my phone. It contained a picture of my former student Amalia[3] with a friend of mine in Chile. That moment, I knew I had to tell the story of Amalia and me as an example of how my understanding of the ACRL Framework has affected my work beyond the film class that was my focus during the co-design workshop.

In the fall of 2017, in addition to collaborating in the film class, I had also taught another first-year class dealing with disciplines in which the information literacy component seemed extremely challenging. I had taught that class twice before, and I always had asked myself how I could do a better job and sometimes even asked myself if information literacy made any sense in this context. Seeing the photograph from Amalia, one of the students in that second course, prompted me to reflect on how the co-design experience had influenced my work in this challenging context as well.

AUP's FirstBridge Structure and Dynamics

FirstBridge is part of the general education program at AUP. Like many other universities across the globe, AUP created a first-year program where students bond around learning communities, which contribute to student retention and ultimately help develop the students' lifelong skills. The name *FirstBridge* comes from the fact that the first semester is a bridge between high school and the university, and it is also associated with the city of Paris, where so many monumental bridges allow the passage between the *Rive Gauche* and the *Rive Droite* of the river Seine. In FirstBridge, students enroll in a pair of courses taught by two professors from two different disciplines, who work as partners to develop a transdisciplinary bridge between those courses. The same group of students meets with each professor separately each week and then once a week again for a common reflective seminar, an opportunity for the two faculty members and the students to reflect on the interdisciplinary connections between both disciplines. In addition, one librarian is assigned to the FirstBridge and meets with the students three to four times per semester during the reflective seminars, as well as outside of class activities. One instance is a FirstBridge dinner in the city or a field trip.

Every September, at the beginning of fall semester, the FirstBridge coordinator organizes the first FirstBridge faculty meeting, an important moment when faculty come revived from their vacation, ready to meet colleagues and share their best moments of the summer. The main purpose of this meeting is to remind faculty of the FirstBridge structure and learning objectives and to facilitate the dialogue of faculty pairings and the librarian assigned to each FirstBridge cohort. Syllabi, schedules, learning objectives, and common activities are discussed. The dates and class periods of the sessions related to information literacy are also discussed with the librarian. The precise dates for these reflective seminars containing information literacy instruction are important because they are linked and scaffolded to particular assignments (oral presentations, bibliographies, research papers, etc.). This first meeting is key as it allows the librarian to communicate and refresh the memory of the faculty in terms of learning outcomes for information literacy and to talk about the integration of the different activities required for every FirstBridge.

For a few consecutive years, a science professor has teamed up with an arts professor, and in September 2017, I had the occasion of meeting with both of these FirstBridge faculty. We developed a week-by-week list of activities, as well as setting the date for the outside-of-class activities: the FirstBridge dinner in the arts professor's *atelier d'artiste* in the outskirts of Paris and a new activity I proposed for that specific semester that would help me better integrate the connections between my section and their disciplines. In a few days' time, both professors had given the final touches to their syllabi and fixed the dates for the reflective seminars. In the fall 2017 semester, our FirstBridge was called Creating: Ways of World Making, which would show the connections between two courses: the Art and Science of Creating Digital Stuff and a drawing and sculpture class. Both courses were based on the notions of creativity, invention, and innovation, and both courses had a common final presentation of the students' projects, which were showcased at the end of the semester along with other FirstBridge classes.

It is important to lay out the learning goals of both classes in order to better visualize the possible integration of the information literacy modules and the potential challenges and difficulties for a librarian.

Creating: Ways of World Making—Learning Goals

The general education program at AUP consisted of four requirements: Speaking the World, Modeling the World, Mapping the World, and Comparing Worlds

Past and Present. This FirstBridge fulfilled the Modeling the World requirement and as such had the following learning objectives:

- Students will learn fundamental 3-D design.
- Students will better understand the materials and techniques for creating 3-D prototypes.
- Students will deepen their appreciation of what has been designed already.

Regarding the Art and Science of Creating Digital Stuff, learning goals included learning how to create simple web pages and computer programs (in the visual Java-based programming tool Scratch). According to the professor, students also will:

- have acquired critical skills to take advantage of modern digital environments,
- have an appreciation of the creative process in the arts and sciences, and
- increase their ability to creatively approach different problems.

Regarding the specific art studio class, learning goals included learning how to create simple 3-D toys and models and simple interactive machines. According to the professor, students also will:

- have acquired critical skills to assess objects designed by others,
- have an appreciation of the creative process in the arts and sciences,
- have an informed opinion about the current state of design and the marketing of design objects, and
- be able to comprehend the connections between creative design and the scientific world in the context of the FirstBridge learning community.

For their final projects, students had to present a small sculpture and a Lego robot and show the progress made.

The core concept of the FirstBridge was creativity. The emphasis was placed on originality and engagement rather than the utility of the objects students produced.

My Information Literacy Challenge

My information literacy challenge was triple. The first challenge was to work with a Framework that seems abstract to me and even more so to my two academic partners. In order to be able to incorporate the frames, I needed to understand them and be able to explain them to my FirstBridge faculty partners.

Secondly, I needed to find opportunities to embed my content and develop relevant activities for our reflective seminars. It was easier in the past with courses requiring literature reviews, bibliographies, blogs, papers, research logs, or presentations for which students needed to look for information, evaluate it, and use it, but in this case I was confronted with a group of students developing small computer programs, starting to get familiar with materials, and modeling them with the goal of creating a piece of artwork or a robot for the end-of-semester project. The mentality of the group of students then is not geared toward writing papers and preparing outlines but rather toward being artistically and scientifically creative. An ambiance of pragmatism had prevailed the previous year, and something creative needed to happen in the way I approached my teaching in order to help with learning. I did not picture myself working in the arts class with clay trying to produce a sculpture and talking about Scholarship as Conversation. The gap between them was too vast, and I needed to find another way of linking the arts and teaching information literacy.

The kinds of skills developed during FirstBridge are key as students go to upper-level classes, and they are expected by faculty. Depriving my group of students of those information literacy and critical-thinking skills would be a mistake. Something needed to change. Adding a new activity at the beginning of the semester helped me on this mission.

Finally, another challenge has been the idea of turning the classroom around and allowing students ownership over the knowledge they will create, giving them an opportunity to construct their own knowledge, especially given the fact that a reflective seminar is not a lecture but a space where students, faculty, and the librarian can reflect. I needed to invite students to develop their information-literate abilities. This third challenge is addressed in more detail in the lesson plan that I present in another section of this work.[4]

The First Weeks of Class

During the orientation week, AUP FirstBridge students met for the first time, and both professors and I spoke to the class in terms of the subjects they had chosen and the information literacy piece that was going to happen. I met the group again that week during the FirstBridge dinner at the *atelier d'artiste* around a salmon BBQ and some wine and cheese. On both occasions, I saw a group of excited new students, all coming from various parts of the world. Usually, at the beginning of the FirstBridge, students tend to gather in comfort-zoned regional groups. This FirstBridge had a few Latin American students who started to talk to me in Spanish, and as a result a certain bond started then with these students.

I spotted Amalia among this group of Latin American students, and we started to talk. Her parents wanted her to go to a liberal arts school with general education requirements, while she was ready for specialization and to go to her major in as little time as possible. This was the first of many interesting one-on-one conversations she and I had about her education, and I was flattered one day because after one of the discussions she told me I was like her art professor, a mentor and a leader to her.

La Off du Design de Paris

In September, parallel to the Paris Design Week, there is another event called *la Off du Design*, which takes place every year in a mythical venue in the city of Paris, the *Cité de la Mode et du Design de Paris* by the Seine river. Students and former students from different French schools of design, as well as young creators, present their prototypes and models applied to industry, business, and arts and crafts. This outside-of-class experience was my opportunity to connect the two courses with the information literacy component, to make it less abstract, and I am thankful to both of my faculty partners for trusting me and allowing me to take the entire FirstBridge group to this big event of design and creation in the city of Paris. On this occasion our FirstBridge students were exposed to vivid and real examples of creation, innovation, invention, and a variety of objects and ideas, ideas that were central to our courses and to the information literacy concepts to be applied later in our reflective seminars. The images and ideas at this event would help me as an instructor to start talking about the different design, innovation, and invention we would discuss in the information literacy sessions.

Creativity as a Conductive Thread

Every FirstBridge group has its own Blackboard site, and there is a section devoted to information literacy with common pre- and post-assessments used by all librarians, web discussions, and exercises on plagiarism and MLA, all uploaded by librarians. In that year, I decided to use examples of websites featuring the designers of the *Off du Design* and their work on our Blackboard site. Students would explore these websites and research the designers from the *Off du Design*. Because I had recently attended the co-design workshop, the Framework was in the back of my mind, but I decided not to share the frames directly with the students. Instead, the discussions, analysis, and web exercises available on the Blackboard site were centered around the notions of creativity, innovation, and invention as the driving concepts. I had decided that for students, the *fil conducteur* (conductive thread) would be the notion of creativity. Creativity would be our bridge between the science, the art, and information literacy. I too decided to be creative. I needed to put this to the test.

The FirstBridge was composed of weekly double-class-period reflective seminars, out of which three were devoted to information literacy, which allowed some very interesting time to develop the students' skills and dispositions toward scholarship and their academic work. Students learned during these reflective seminars how to brainstorm and how to use mind maps as a way to start doing research. They developed an outline and started a literature review all around art and creativity, robotics and creation, and invention and innovation.

Although not addressed explicitly, the FirstBridge related to the ACRL Framework when dealing with creativity and creation. The concepts from the Framework would govern the experience, especially Scholarship as Conversation and Information Creation as a Process. In particular, students explored concepts including authorship of each creation, ownership, intellectual property, understanding personal online identity, creation, presenting, representing inspiration, and the use of another person's creativity as a base of one's creation. In the reflective seminars students understood that information has power and generates power. They also understood the importance of selecting and evaluating information and information sources; they dived into the discussion of the creative process, invention, innovation, and inspiration, as well as plagiarism.

During the first information literacy session, students evaluated the websites and compared the types of information available on the web and contrasted them with our online resources. For example, the class looked up the definitions of *invention*, *innovation*, *creation*, *recreating*, *use and reuse*, and *design*. The group identified the definitions that seemed more scholarly and adopted them before moving on to other discussions. In a later session, we discussed and contrasted types of sources depending on the kind of class assignment required by their professors. Students also became aware of the fact that they can contribute to a scholarly conversation, as well as being part of the world of art by creating their own sculptures. During the last session we spoke about plagiarism and the need for citing sources or acknowledging the source of inspiration when the student is inspired by a previous artist, or by an industrial design in the case of the robot construction. In all these sessions the main frames were present in the background and as part of our academic activity.

During the last session, students were invited to do the common information literacy post-assessment, and progress was made by most students. On the pre-assessment they had given feedback about knowing how to use databases and how to use library resources in an effective way. When asked if they had learned what they hoped, most of them agreed. To be honest, however, some students did not see the connection between a model, a sculpture, and the process of creation and authorship.

After this FirstBridge, the story of Amalia and the other Latin American students in that cohort continued. Slowly during the FirstBridge, I noticed Amalia's expression of surprise as she was exposed to all the interdisciplinary content of our courses. This attitude was corroborated later in her following semesters. Like the Spanish fan, once it is open you realize how large the spectrum can be and how much one ignores. Once the Spanish fan opens and the student is curious, they will likely react in a positive way. Amalia was one of those students.

Some of the students from this FirstBridge came for research help during the following semesters. During FirstBridge one starts seeing students come to the library to work and do homework. The library becomes one of their landmarks and territories on campus. Amalia and her Latin American friends were among these students, and they came a few times with reference questions. It became very pleasant to see these young, smiling, positive-thinking, and curious students come for reference help. We often talked about what librarians do with their patrons, mind mapping, outlines, keywords, databases, and books and e-books, as well as citing sources. It became clear to me how their attitude toward research and information literacy had changed and their level of knowledge had evolved.

Amalia and Information Creation as a Process

Amalia came to see me one semester later. She had joined a journalism class, and she needed to interview the person of her choice with the hope of being published in one of the student newspapers. I agreed to be interviewed by her, and we made an appointment. On the day of our interview I was surprised that Amalia did not have a recording device with her, leaving me with a certain hesitation about how accurate her notes might be. However, the interview was a real pleasure. Amalia asked me so many questions about my personal and professional life that opening up to her became pleasant and comforting. The human contact was of great quality. I was happy because I found inspiration and content for a good story; she left also happy as she had a good story to write about …from her notes.

Weeks later the interview appeared in the AUP student newspaper. I was sure Amalia got a good grasp of the majority of the content, but something must have happened between the note taking and the writing of the article, or perhaps the session with the editor, because the story was not my story. Words in quotation marks were definitely not mine; facts, chronology, and words were changed in the article. I had suddenly lost faith in the lessons spent on citation, plagiarism, and intellectual integrity. How can a whole first semester of information literacy be forgotten or overlooked so fast? I cannot deny the fact that the idea of the frames Scholarship as Conversation and Information Creation as a Process as dispositions crossed my mind several times that day. The direction of the interview, as well as the questions, were very bright, but the deeper understanding of the basics of the frames had been left aside.

A few days later I ran into the professor who taught the journalism class, under whose responsibility Amalia had written the article, and I expressed my dissatisfaction. My faculty colleague assured me that he needed to have a conversation on intellectual honesty and good practices with her. I knew I was probably risking my fragile friendship with Amalia.

Weeks later Amalia came to the library, and as she exited the main gate I called her name, and I had no answer. Amalia kept walking firmly away from the university library. I was very sad; my desire to have my professional image restored and the intention of having her learn about academic best practices had sacrificed our friendship. I thought about it more as a human being and not as a professional. I had lost a friend.

Months later, the time of AUP's World's Fairs arrived, and the office of Student Development had asked me if I, as an Ecuadorian, could help the Ecuadorian table present their culinary specialties. At that event Amalia was at her nation's table inviting everyone to have a taste of their delicacies. Of course, I tasted some of her homemade food, which she had made following her family recipes, and it was then that she told me that she was not at all mad at me. She had probably had music on her headphones, as that is what she does when leaving the library. The conversation with her professor had happened, and her next articles were of much higher quality. Research help conversations with the librarians continued afterward. I insist that learning about information literacy is a process that should not take place only in the classroom, but also outside of it, while conducting interviews, while doing an internship, and so on.

In her second year Amalia opted for a one-year-abroad experience in South America, and I had no further news on her until the Saturday morning when I was thinking of the possible chapter for this book and I got a Facebook Messenger text from a friend of mine from high school now working as a human rights professor and activist in South America. The text message was followed by a picture of him with Amalia! He had been asked by a group of American universities in his town to give a talk on the state of human rights in the South American region and the objectives of sustainable development of the region. My friend and Amalia decided after the conference to send me their selfie on the spot. So there she is, our Global Explorer around the world getting a richer experience, and I am hoping that the conversations about Information Creation as a Process, Scholarship as Conversation, and Authority is Constructed and Contextual will follow her during her student life and further as a professional.

When I reflect back on the moment when I received this selfie, I remember there was not only the emotional part but also the reflection on how I had changed my own teaching using discipline-related concepts—such as innovation, creation, and invention—with the Framework in the back of my mind and hoping that the course learning goals would be met. These memories brought me even further back to the AMICAL workshop that had transformed me as an instructor.

I look forward to meeting Amalia again to observe if and how the information literacy threshold concepts have been irreversible or transformative. What is true to me is that her disposition toward information gathering and creation have evolved.

I purposefully wanted to have a connecting relationship with some of our students, and Amalia is one example. This is not only from the personal side, but also to see the possible impact my instruction may have in their lives and to observe if there is a transformative process. This specific experience confirmed that information literacy, including the Framework, is not something that needs to or can happen punctually during the first year but rather across the student's life while in college. It needs a follow-up. The student and the librarian need to have certain contact throughout the student's career.

Conclusion

At the end of the semester, the FirstBridge students presented their final projects: robots made with Legos or their sculptures. They also took the information literacy post-assessment, which showed encouraging progress. I noticed that their level of information literacy relates more to specific skills and competencies than to predispositions toward information, which is what the Framework tries to provoke in students. The group of AUP librarians has stopped using these homemade FirstBridge pre- and post-assessment surveys based on the ACRL standards.[5] Two of us started a pilot trying to adapt both surveys to the Framework. Students took the new post-assessment, but we still have a long way to go to test the new tool and see if it will be adopted by other colleagues in future years.

For the Framework to work successfully, information literacy needs to be followed up and monitored at upper levels. After my years of experience and from my personal observation, I am convinced that students who have had various information literacy modules during the first semester, as is the case in FirstBridge, always have a better understanding of and a better predisposition toward research and information than transfer students who were not exposed to these sessions. However, when it comes to developing attitudes and dispositions, such as those discussed in the Framework, those start being acquired only in higher-level courses and as a second or third layer of information literacy, at a second stage of experience when research has become more of a habit and students reflect more maturity. Perhaps we can allow ourselves to talk about the success or failure of librarians working with the Framework only when students graduate, at the capstone level.

For me the Framework remains aspirational. There are by now some interesting tools developed by colleagues that can be viewed in the Framework for Information Literacy Sandbox, Project CORA, or 23 Framework Things that can help librarians get more comfortable with this document.[6] I think I will continue making progress once the Framework becomes more and more familiar. I hope I will take the Framework to my teaching 2.0 stage along with new pedagogies.

I believe that assessing the impact of the Framework can be done only diachronically, meaning through the entire life span of a student. It is very difficult to assess limited to a specific semester, and therefore the methods of evaluation need to be more imaginative and creative. How to implement an information literacy program through a student's career when having one-shot classes seems to be the rule on most campuses internationally? For the Framework to work, every college and university will have to develop a more ambitious information literacy program across the curriculum.

My original question remains: can the ACRL Framework be taught at the first-year level given the maturity of college students at this point? Also, is it useful in some discipline-specific cases such as art, computer science, sciences, and even robotics? I like the fact that the ACRL Framework allows librarians more local and course-specific adaptation, and I found it useful in the courses I discuss here. Librarians can teach with the concepts in the Framework once they have internalized the Framework. On the other hand, when it comes to explaining what librarians do with these frames, trying to engage students and faculty around the Framework can be perceived as esoteric; it builds a communication barrier with our partners. My personal technique has been to try to explain the Framework with more natural language and even non-Framework vocabulary—if not, our field is perceived as full of jargon.

The co-design workshop had a very positive impact for my faculty partner and me at the time. She and I improved the course design by developing disciplinary learning goals for her as well as goals for my information literacy sessions. Both had the opportunity to develop our course with the Framework. During this film course and the FirstBridge that I taught in this same semester, I lost my own apprehension toward the new ACRL Framework.

Amalia is back on campus now. We have touched base and made explicit our intention to work together for reference questions or anything concerning information literacy or research methodology. I hope that I will have the opportunity to follow up on her predispositions toward information and scholarly work. I now see many more students like Amalia on campus, students who come to study in Paris with us. I hope to be able to contribute to their academic careers from my position as information literacy librarian.

Notes

1. Association of College and Research Libraries, *Framework for Information Literacy for Higher Education* (Chicago: Association of College and Research Libraries, 2016).
2. Samantha Godbey and Xan Goodman, "Co-design: Integrating Information Literacy into Your Disciplinary Course" (AMICAL workshop, American University of Paris, March 31–April 1, 2017), https://www.amicalnet.org/events/co-design-integrating-information-literacy-into-your-disciplinary-course.
3. Name has been changed.
4. See the lesson plan "Exploring Creativity, Innovation, and Invention."
5. Association of College and Research Libraries, *Information Literacy Competency Standards for Higher Education* (Chicago: Association of College and Research Libraries, 2000).
6. ACRL Framework for Information Literacy Sandbox home page, Association of College and Research Libraries, https://sandbox.acrl.org/; CORA: Community of Online Research Assignments, Loyola Marymount University Library, https://www.projectcora.org/; 23 Framework Things, https://23frameworkthings.wordpress.com/.

Bibliography

Association of College and Research Libraries. ACRL Framework for Information Literacy Sandbox home page. https://sandbox.acrl.org/.

———. *Framework for Information Literacy for Higher Education*. Chicago: Association of College and Research Libraries, 2016.

———. *Information Literacy Competency Standards for Higher Education*. Chicago: Association of College and Research Libraries, 2000.

Godbey, Samantha, and Xan Goodman. "Co-design: Integrating Information Literacy into Your Disciplinary Course." AMICAL workshop, American University of Paris, March 31–April 1, 2017. https://www.amicalnet.org/events/co-design-integrating-information-literacy-into-your-disciplinary-course.

Loyola Marymount University Library. CORA: Community of Online Research Assignments home page. https://www.projectcora.org/.

23 Framework Things home page. https://23frameworkthings.wordpress.com/.

CASE STUDY 6

Co-designing an Information Literacy Experience for Non-textual Assignments in a Public Speaking Course

Ivana Stevanović

Institutional Librarian, RIT Kosovo (A.U.K), Kosovo

This collaboration is a result of an initiative started in 2015,[1] when I, the author, experimented with possibility of tracing and successfully triggering metaliteracy at the freshman level, with specific regard to metacognition. The experiment involved looking at different points of assessment and associated assignments for a twentieth-century history course, based on the ACRL *Framework for Information Literacy for Higher Education.*[2]

For this project Dr. Linda Ziberi and I decided to include information literacy in her public speaking course to enhance and confirm the essential role that information literacy instruction can play in guiding and developing student independent thinking and learning. With lessons learned from a previous project, we wanted to look further at proper strategies for connecting information literacy and metaliteracy. We sought to connect specific frames from the Framework with course assignments to demonstrate that application of knowledge had happened. The challenge, and our wish, was to create a descriptive assessment applicable not only to textual works, but also to other forms of assignments.

The nature of the public speaking course for which this faculty-librarian collaboration was planned made collaborating interesting and unique. While researching existing scholarship, we found a limited number of works addressing experiences that include information literacy in oral communication courses.[3]

Dr. Ziberi and I see faculty-librarian collaboration as an effort to embed information literacy into a course and specifically to work together on information literacy assessment from the perspective that information literacy is not an entirely separate discipline. Furthermore, faculty, and our university in general, are already aiming to nurture a student who is an active learner and an independent thinker, who is curious and critical about the world. Information literacy in our university context involves an approach that allows teaching and nurturing metaliteracy education in a systematic way.

We began with the idea that information literacy offers a systematic line of action to nurturing and encouraging the general goals and mission of higher education, so we collaborated to develop content for the existing public speaking course syllabus to add an information literacy component. We placed a strong emphasis on the librarian and library resources visibility within the syllabus, so information literacy became an integral part of instruction and assessment. There were four major points of discussion during our planning process: a student sample, information literacy lessons, assessment, and a final assignment assessment using a jointly created faculty-librarian information literacy rubric. We had one major concern arising from the project evaluation discussion, and that was long-term sustainability of these initiatives.

Our initial lesson included five frames from the Framework since we could identify elements of almost each of the frames present to some degree in our lesson plan and overall goals. In the end, we selected two frames as our primary focus. We think no information literacy projects can be holistic if most, or all, of the six frames are not incorporated throughout the information literacy instruction to a certain degree. For instance, in addition to our two selected frames, Information Creation as a Process and Authority Is Constructed and Contextual, I also think Research as Inquiry, Searching as Strategic Exploration, and Information Has Value are impossible not to touch upon during our information literacy sessions.

The public speaking course was taught in fall semester 2017. All students were first-year, or recent high school graduates, with no or only very basic information literacy experience; they were also non-native English speakers. Dr. Ziberi taught two sections; we decided to use one section as a control group. One section was exposed to the new information literacy plan, while the other section had the usual information literacy plan. The usual information literacy plan allowed for a single one-shot library instruction session during week four.

Integrating Information Literacy into the Public Speaking Course

Our second major conversation point during the planning process was how to deliver the information literacy lesson plans. With the information literacy outcomes that we created for this course, we were concerned about being able to actually complete everything that must precede insight into student metacognition, especially if we had only a one-time session available for information literacy. Metacognitive processes take time and repetition in different situations to develop and become constant. In order to reach metacognition, students need to master a certain skill level of information literacy. We had to ensure that the full scope of skills (or at least those essential to our outcomes) related to understanding, selecting, and evaluating information was covered in a timely way.

We devised information literacy lessons utilizing a flipped classroom model by means of online tutorials, individual consultations, and in-class information literacy sessions. Borrowing from our partner institution, Rochester Institute of Technology (RIT), we used six online tutorials that matched our information literacy lesson plan:

- #1: Identifying Sources
- #2: Choosing a Topic
- #4: Finding Articles
- #5: Using the Web
- #7: Plagiarism & Copyright
- #8: Citing Sources

These tutorial sessions were self-paced, web-based sessions to be completed during weeks four, five, and seven. Students were to watch a prerecorded tutorial and complete a quiz by a given deadline. All online sessions were listed in the syllabus, along with links to the tutorials.

The in-class information literacy session was held during week six for one hour. Individual consultations with a librarian were also listed in the syllabus, and students were expected to attend at least one consultation.

We revised the assignments to integrate information literacy. Students were required to complete a group informative speech for 15 percent of their final grade and an individual persuasive speech for 20 percent of their final grade. Five percent of the grade for each of these two speeches comes from information literacy assessments integrated into the speech preparation. An additional 10 percent of their final grade was based on an information literacy reflective essay assignment. Students were also awarded participation points for completing the online tutorials and for attending the in-class information literacy sessions.

Our co-designed information literacy sessions included library instruction that was scheduled with the close consideration of when assignments were due to maximize student exposure to information literacy elements in their assignments. We deliberately scaffolded instruction to use the informative speech assignment as a practice for information gathering and later reinforced information literacy with the persuasive speech assignment. This arc allowed students to demonstrate their retention and application of information literacy practices throughout the course.

Assessments

We decided to use a course portfolio as our information literacy assessment method. To fully assess metacognition we utilized Proformas (structured template documents) for both speech assignments, online tutorial quizzes, an outline for the persuasive speech, and the information literacy reflective essay. Students were also required to keep weekly journals for the duration of the course. The portfolio allowed us to see evidence of student self-reflection and metacognitive processes. Other elements of the portfolio, such as planning for the group informative speech, required students to report on search strategies they used to locate and select resources for their speech. We adapted the speech Proformas from Valerie Sonley, Denise Turner, Sue Myer, and Yvonne Cotton's information literacy module at the University of Teesside in the United Kingdom.[4] Their Proforma is based on Empire State College's research portfolio use.

The reflective essay encouraged students to be more aware of their learning process and their progress with information literacy. Students completed the reflective essay at the end of the semester by answering a set of guided questions. This assignment was not graded. We were interested only in seeing evidence of students' self-evaluation of their learning process.

Information literacy assignments were planned to allow a gradual and step-by-step insight into the learning process. Each quiz that students took after watching the information literacy tutorials could be redone multiple times before submitting the final version. The idea of the quizzes was not to grade them, but to review students' understanding and retention of the concepts covered by each of the tutorials.

Dr. Ziberi and I wanted to develop a rubric based on a number of the recommendations in the AAC&U VALUE Rubrics to assess the persuasive speech based on the frames Information Creation as a Process and Authority Is Constructed and Contextual.[5] Our initial desire and opinion was that we would need this information literacy assessment point because it would wrap up nicely the whole assessment process and show evidence of metacognition taking place. We based this on my experience with a previous history project. After a number of conversations and reflections on the matter, I began to ask if it were categorically important that Dr. Ziberi and I could confirm that these processes are taking place if students were reporting that this is happening in their self-reflection essays. If the ultimate goal of this project was to trace and successfully trigger metaliteracy development, was our stance—that we would define and determine, even quantify, what this is and how much is enough—the right one?

As a result of this thinking, Dr. Ziberi and I concluded that as long as we were able to read a student self-report on their transformation and change, it was unimportant to use a rubric to attempt to define and scale levels of metacognition. For assessment purposes we decided our focus for this project should be on the reflective essay or diary to determine if metacognition happened for the students during the course. We were also worried about the amount of time needed to create a rubric and that we might fail since we were already engaged in an ambitious plan.

Sustaining Co-design

Overall, Dr. Ziberi and I greatly enjoyed the whole co-designing collaboration. Our dynamics prior to, during, and after the course have provided a fertile ground for continuous professional and personal advancement. We have both experienced transformation and changes in our perceptions in how we see the public speaking course, our roles, and learning outcomes. Interacting with a professional from a different field who has different understandings and definitions for similar concepts has altered some of what we see as our own disciplinary threshold concepts. We both think differently now about teaching pedagogy, oral communication, information literacy, and assessment, and this is all because of our collaboration. The whole experience sparked curiosity and fun within both of us, taking us sometimes to exceptionally ambitious, creative, and innovative ideas about how to co-design and redesign in the future semesters.

Even though we both enjoyed this experience, and we saw evidence of students' increased quality of work, Dr. Ziberi and I did not continue our project in succeeding semesters. Co-designing presents challenges with sustainability and continuity for projects of this size and nature because institutions have varying levels of resources to sustain collaborative endeavors. Information literacy instruction is not a mandatory curriculum requirement in our institution. This means that continuous presence of projects of this kind is dependent on the individual, rather than systematic endeavor. Given that most of our faculty have a substantial teaching load, it is challenging to transform interest into a sustainable co-design project. In addition, the workload added to the librarian included extra working hours. This was a significant addition to my regular duties, which had to remain intact to ensure no lapse in the quality of service outside of this collaboration.

A Successful Co-design Experience: Pre-Paris

Co-designing can be successful, as I will share briefly about a co-design experience that occurred two years prior to the co-design Paris workshop.[6] In 2015 I successfully collaborated with a history professor to include information literacy in his course. After our co-designing project for Dr. Benson's history course, he returned to his home institution, Cornerstone University (CU), where he continued similar projects. Here I present a brief reflection prepared by Dr. Benson and Ms. Bolger, a librarian, on projects they continued and their impact. Dr. Benson and Ms. Bolger's work changed their whole institutional perception about information literacy instruction. Below is their experience:

> *Upon returning to his home institution, Benson approached the library staff about continuing the initiative in his history courses at CU. Gina Bolger, the library's history liaison, partnered with him to implement it. Over the last three years they have further developed the assignment, making it a fixture in a number of CU's history courses. The first stage of the assignment requires students to meet with the librarians early in the semester to develop their topics, learn how to find appropriate sources, and begin research. In the next stage, the students submit project proposals with an embedded bibliography which is graded by the librarians. The librarians also grade the bibliographic element of the research paper, which is the final stage of the project. As they have worked with the assignment, Benson and Bolger have made some refinements. For example, the librarians' initial research consultation with the students is now done in small groups of four students or less, rather than in larger groups. Many students have commented that this has made the sessions more individualized and helpful, and has made them more comfortable with using the library databases for research. Overall, the results have been remarkable, with dramatic improvements in the quality of the sources used in student research. This has been substantiated by data collected through surveys as well as grades.*
>
> *This model has been so successful that other librarians at CU have begun to implement it in their liaison areas. The Teacher Education and Business programs now have embedded librarians in their classes and have seen improvement in the academic quality of research papers. As with the history classes, data have shown that the students who have participated in this process have been able to apply these skills in classes across disciplines.*

What began with a simple request over three years ago has led to a remarkably fruitful collaborative effort, one that has spanned oceans but also institutions and disciplines. It has been a very positive experience, showing what is possible when faculty and librarians collaborate to improve student information literacy and learning.

Conclusion

The ACRL *Framework for Information Literacy for Higher Education* has provided productive ground for an exploration of information literacy teaching outcomes, which grasp higher order abilities and intertwine and match with the lifelong learning goals a university strives to inspire among students. The Framework has enabled a faculty-librarian communication that can lead to more opportunities for common ground and understanding, especially in regard to learning goals. Although the amount of time needed for developing and implementing a co-designing initiative directly influences the sustainability of these projects, I end this reflective article with hopes that the remarkable benefits to student learning experience, as well as the opportunity for professional and personal development, will encourage more colleagues to try at least once this pedagogical and intellectual adventure.

Notes

1. For the lesson plan from the history course project, see "A Historical Experiment in Historic Time: A Collaborative Effort toward a Different Information Literacy Experience" in this book.
2. Association of College and Research Libraries, *Framework for Information Literacy for Higher Education* (Chicago: Association of College and Research Libraries, 2016).
3. The two we could find corresponding to what we were interested in were Lisa M. Sjoberg and Stephanie L. Ahlfeldt, "Bridging the Gap: Integrating Information Literacy into Communication Courses," *Communication Teacher* 24, no. 3 (2010): 131–35 and Kari D. Weaver and Penni M. Pier, "Embedded Information Literacy in the Basic Oral Communication Course: From Conception through Assessment," *Public Services Quarterly* 6, no. 2–3 (2010): 259–70, https://doi.org/10.1080/15228959.2010.497455.
4. Valerie Sonley et al., "Information Literacy Assessment by Portfolio: A Case Study," *Reference Services Review* 35, no. 1 (2007): 41–70, https://doi.org/10.1108/00907320710729355.

5. Association of American Colleges and Universities, "VALUE Rubrics," https://www.aacu.org/value-rubrics.
6. Samantha Godbey and Xan Goodman, "Co-design: Integrating Information Literacy into Your Disciplinary Course" (AMICAL workshop, American University of Paris, March 31–April 1, 2017), https://www.amicalnet.org/events/co-design-integrating-information-literacy-into-your-disciplinary-course.

Bibliography

Association of American Colleges and Universities. "VALUE Rubrics." https://www.aacu.org/value-rubrics.

Association of College and Research Libraries. *Framework for Information Literacy for Higher Education*. Chicago: Association of College and Research Libraries, 2016.

Godbey, Samantha, and Xan Goodman. "Co-design: Integrating Information Literacy into Your Disciplinary Course." AMICAL workshop, American University of Paris, March 31–April 1, 2017. https://www.amicalnet.org/events/co-design-integrating-information-literacy-into-your-disciplinary-course.

Rochester Institute of Technology Libraries. "Learning Information Veracity @ RIT." https://library.rit.edu/liv/.

Sjoberg, Lisa M., and Stephanie L. Ahlfeldt. "Bridging the Gap: Integrating Information Literacy into Communication Courses." *Communication Teacher* 24, no. 3 (2010): 131–35.

Sonley, Valerie, Denise Turner, Sue Myer, and Yvonne Cotton. "Information Literacy Assessment by Portfolio: A Case Study." *Reference Services Review* 35, no. 1 (2007): 41–70. https://doi.org/10.1108/00907320710729355.

Weaver, Kari D., and Penni M. Pier. "Embedded Information Literacy in the Basic Oral Communication Course: From Conception through Assessment." *Public Services Quarterly* 6, no. 2–3 (2010): 259–70. https://doi.org/10.1080/15228959.2010.497455.

CASE STUDY 7

Redesigning a Writing-Intensive Graduate Course

An Information Literacy Case Study at AUB

Najla Jarkas, PhD
Senior Lecturer, English Department, American University of Beirut, Lebanon

Fatmeh Charafeddine
Associate University Librarian, Research and Academic Collaboration Services, University Libraries, American University of Beirut, Lebanon

Introduction

In spring 2017, Dr. Najla Jarkas, senior lecturer in the English Department, and Fatmeh Charafeddine, research and instruction librarian at the University Libraries of the American University of Beirut, joined the two-day co-design workshop at the American University of Paris (AUP) in order to learn ways of integrating aspects of the ACRL *Framework for Information Literacy for Higher Education* into a disciplinary course.[1] The faculty and librarians revised course learning outcomes, assignments, and assessments and developed an implementation plan to identify when and in which way the librarian would contribute to the course.

Accordingly, in fall 2017, Dr. Jarkas and Ms. Charafeddine prepared and offered a co-designed pilot course for English 300: Writing in the Disciplines at the American University of Beirut. The following will discuss how the co-design process took effect and what challenges and factors impacted the dynamics in the relationship between the instructor and the librarian.

Setting and Context

Founded in 1866, the American University of Beirut (AUB) is one of the oldest universities in the Arab region that follow the American liberal arts model of higher education. In the Middle East and North Africa region, AUB is predated only by Robert College in Istanbul, founded in 1863. Starting off as a male-only university, AUB became coeducational in 1922 and is at present 48 percent male and 52 percent female. Twenty-two percent of AUB's students are international, coming from at least ninety countries. The main language of instruction is English, except for some of the courses that are taught in the Arabic department, in addition to other language courses. The university offers up to 130 programs to a body of 7,180 undergraduate students and 1,922 graduate students. With a ratio of eleven students to each faculty member, the university employs 903 full-time instructional faculty and 293 part-time instructional faculty.[2]

The focus of the university is teaching and research, and AUB strongly prides itself on being rooted in western notions of freedom of thought and expression, respect for diversity and tolerance, commitment "to creative and critical thinking, life-long learning, personal integrity, civic responsibility, and leadership,"[3] which is very appealing to the young students in the region.

AUB is regarded as one of the most prestigious universities in the country as well as in neighboring countries in the region such as Syria, Jordan, Palestine, and the Arabian Gulf. AUB constantly appears among the most highly rated universities in the QS Arab region rankings (the most widely used university ranking system in the region);[4] indeed, in 2018 it achieved the first rank. Students look at it as an example of excellence in teaching that will open up future prospects and prestigious careers. A degree from AUB is perceived as the gateway, certainly guaranteeing a good job and a professional career. The broad-based liberal arts education at AUB plays a role in building this prestigious reputation, in addition to the research and reputation of its local and international faculty.

The university also prides itself on possessing in its libraries one of the largest collections of books, journals, and databases in the region.

Information Literacy at AUB

The Research and Instruction Services Department at the University Libraries runs a long-standing information literacy program. The program started with the creation of the Information Services Department at the University Libraries in 2002. The department aimed to strategize and organize the University Libraries' efforts of marketing the growing e-resources collection, providing outreach, and offering library instruction sessions. Among the department's major achievements was partnering in organizing the Andrew W. Mellon Summer Seminar on Creative Use of Resources starting in the summer of 2004. This seminar was part of the University Teaching Excellence initiative, and it was intended to assist faculty in making further use of various academic resources available and integrating those resources in the development of specific courses. The three main areas of integration were curriculum design, library information services, and educational technology tools (WebCT).

The six-week summer seminar was offered for five consecutive years from 2004 to 2008. Each seminar was attended by about fourteen faculty members from different disciplines. The seminar aimed to provide faculty with the technical skills necessary to incorporate technology in their teaching process and to include a library and information literacy component in their class in order to enhance the effective use of the library's growing electronic resources collection. Fatmeh Charafeddine was then the e-resources librarian and was instrumental in involving librarians in outreach and instruction activities at the university level. The cost of e-resources subscriptions was skyrocketing while the library was receiving inquiries from students not aware of the rich collections the library was acquiring. This discrepancy was very disturbing to the library administration, who strongly advocated the need to introduce library instruction and information literacy to AUB.

The summer seminar program was a great opportunity to start the integration of the library services and collections in the teaching and learning process at the university. The Information Services Department has continued to enhance its program; in 2011, it merged with the Reference Department to become the Research and Instruction Services Department under the leadership of

Ms. Charafeddine and has maintained a well-established partnership with the Communications Skills Program, offering an average of 800 library sessions for 5,000 students a year. Research and Instruction Services also expanded its services to become a partner with the Graduate Council and the Writing Center at AUB, offering a five-session graduate seminar series every year. Lately, Research and Instruction Services has been focusing on providing specialized services offered by subject librarians and started experimenting with embedded librarian services, which have proven to be very popular but also very demanding.

The department has used the ACRL *Framework for Information Literacy for Higher Education* as a guiding structure since it was adopted by ACRL in 2016. Attending the co-design workshop at AUP was a great opportunity for the department to start offering collaboratively designed information literacy sessions. After the workshop, we discussed how the concepts in the ACRL Framework could help in realizing the co-designed course outcome. We both acknowledged that the threshold concepts of the Framework are broad, theoretical, and sometimes overlapping. While the ACRL Framework is organized around six frames, each focusing on one threshold concept, it does not provide learning outcomes for the concepts in the frame. We needed to transform those concepts into some type of learning outcomes that we could use in the course. We decided to give assignments at the end of each session aligned with the targeted concepts and relevant to the coursework. While co-designing the lessons with the broader frames in mind, we also kept in mind the basics of what students need to know to become information-literate: how to find and select information; how to determine the validity, reliability, and accuracy of information; and how to use information responsibly. Our co-designed course was offered in fall 2017.

Course Co-design

The course chosen for the redesign project, Writing in the Disciplines, is primarily offered to students joining AUB for a graduate degree who could not meet the required English proficiency level set by AUB for graduate studies. Having graduated from schools other than AUB, these students come with a variety of cultural and educational backgrounds, which, as will be discussed later, impacted the results of integrating the ACRL Framework into a new syllabus. Notwithstanding this challenge, this course is extremely important as one of the first graduate courses taken by mostly foreign students during their first graduate semester at

AUB. In fall 2017, the class had fifteen students. The following course description, outcomes, and assignments represent the revised content of the course.

Course Description

Writing in the Disciplines is a fourteen-week course designed to assist students with their graduate-level writing in English. The course begins with a broad-based introduction to academic writing and then moves to discipline-specific research projects. The readings and writing projects help students identify some of the rhetorical moves scholars make as they pose problems, design and conduct research, report data, and draw conclusions. Students also have opportunities to reflect, both formally and informally, on their own writing process as well as on classmates' drafts. The class also works closely with AUB's librarians on information literacy skills and concepts including locating resources, discussing search techniques and strategies, evaluating information, understanding copyright issues, producing information of various types and processes , and considering the ways scholars work collaboratively and deal with issues of intellectual property and plagiarism. Students engage in learning more about the ways reading and writing construct various disciplines. This is a fail-or-pass noncredit course.

Course Learning Outcomes and Integration of the ACRL Framework

The course learning outcomes for Writing in the Disciplines integrating the ACRL Framework are as follows:

- Read, evaluate, and respond critically to academic texts.
  Frames: Authority Is Constructed and Contextual; Information Creation as a Process
- Identify features of disciplinary discourse in your field.
  Frames: Scholarship as Conversation; Research as Inquiry
- Use academic writing style appropriately.
  Frames: Information Has Value; Authority Is Constructed and Contextual

- Evaluate information sources and identify the appropriate sources.
  Frames: Authority Is Constructed and Contextual; Information Creation as a Process; Information Has Value
- Treat research as a conversation, recognizing and crediting previous scholarly work.
  Frames: Scholarship as Conversation; Information Has Value

Assignments

The assignments for this course gradually lead to the final assignment of the research paper. The library sessions needed, as a result, to be designed to support the gradual and iterative process of writing a research paper as the graduate students develop skills in English writing as well as research.

The writing assignments in this course have been revised and modified to integrate four short information literacy assignments aiming to make students familiar with the different types of library resources, how to assess available resources, and how to use resources effectively and responsibly:[5]

- Library Assignment Task 1 (Getting Started with Your Graduate Research): Locate published material in your field from different points of view and publication types.
- Library Assignment Task 2 (Research in the Discipline): Search subject databases, library tools, and reference titles in your field.
- Library Assignment Task 3 (Search Strategies): Come up with keywords and search strategies to best locate sources specific to your topic.
- Library Assignment Task 4 (Assess Information Credibility): Compile an annotated bibliography with different types of resources relevant to your search, and give your assessment of each source.

The Research Paper

One of the major assignments required of all students in this course is the term paper, which incorporates all of the previous smaller assignments. In this assignment students are divided into groups according to their academic major and are asked to collaborate in writing a multidisciplinary research paper relevant to their majors.

Information Literacy Component

It was agreed to offer four library sessions to integrate information literacy concepts into the English 300 class, matching them with the course materials and learning outcomes. The challenge was to also address the different educational, writing, and research needs for this course alongside very basic information literacy needs, such as simply navigating the library website, understanding different resources types, and appropriately citing relevant sources in academic writing. Therefore, a needs assessment survey was distributed to the students at the beginning of week 1 to identify, as much as possible, the areas that need to be addressed in the redesign process of the course. As a result, the four library sessions shown in table CS7.1 were prepared for the course.[6]

Table CS7.1

Library sessions in English 300

Week	Library Sessions	Matching ACRL Framework Concepts
Week 2	Getting Started with Graduate Research	Information Creation as a Process Information Has Value
Week 3	Research in the Discipline	Scholarship as Conversation Authority Is Constructed and Contextual Searching as Strategic Exploration
Week 7	Search Strategies	Searching as Strategic Exploration
Week 8	Information Credibility	Authority Is Constructed and Contextual Information Has Value

Librarian-Faculty Relationships during and after the Co-design Workshop

A number of factors and challenges impacted the dynamics in the relationship between the instructor and librarian as follows. The relationship between the librarian and the instructor developed beyond the traditional notion of librarians at the service of faculty and students. Because the instructor and the librarian had undertaken the journey together to Paris to attend the co-design workshop, the relationship was built on equity and co-teaching principles. The workshop opened the opportunity for both parties to learn from each other and reach a common language that enabled them to co-design the syllabus and understand the challenges and opportunities of implementing new changes to an already established syllabus that the faculty member was previously comfortable teaching. Equity was predominant during the restructuring of the timetable, especially given that the course load was a constant pressure on the faculty member, who had previously depended on a one-time holistic library session for all students attending the course. However, after the faculty member had undergone the training and had established a working relationship with the librarian, the new changes had to be implemented to allow the information literacy concepts to be effectively integrated into the weekly schedule of the writing-intensive course.

To avoid wasting the librarian's time, a factor that can contribute to a more equitable relationship between faculty and librarian is to share the syllabus well ahead of time and freely exchange ideas about the new assignments, order of hands-on sessions, and dates of sessions. Discussions were also undertaken as to what type of new assignments needed to be integrated before and at the end of each information literacy session commensurate with the sequencing of other course assignments. Old course assignments also had to be redesigned and sometimes totally altered in the process upon the request of the librarian to allow for the organic integration of the ACRL Framework. The Framework proved to be an efficient guideline in this process and supportive of the main learning outcomes of the course, as shown in the learning outcomes section above. The reinforcement of the concepts in the ACRL Framework through live discussions in the classroom, followed by practical hands-on exercises and graded assignments, was of crucial importance. The faculty member had to allow for this extra time to be added to the weekly schedule.

Challenges to the Implementation of the Co-design Process

The faculty member teaching this graduate writing-intensive course found the Framework to be better structured and more focused on concepts directly concerned with information literacy in terms of production, dissemination, access, and use, as opposed to the ACRL Standards, which were more focused on the information-seeking cycle as part of the whole process of doing research.[7] Each of the six frames in the Framework is strictly related to understanding of information as a product relevant to researchers and has its own process of creation and accumulation, its special characteristics, ownership rights and rules of sharing and using, ways of searching and finding information, and criteria for assessing and selecting information. Nevertheless, the following challenges arose while trying to integrate the Framework in the class work:

1. **The student cohort:** One of the most significant challenges to the implementation of the co-designed course came from the student cohort. The students were not only total newcomers to AUB and, in some cases, to the country, but were also newcomers to an institution where English is the main language of instruction. Having not been in contact with librarians for support in their previous institutions, they did not identify the librarian as their main source of information, and not all contacted the librarian for any academic support out of the classroom. Moreover, this cohort had to grapple with writing in a language not their own. Class time during and outside the information literacy sessions was spent on orienting students to writing and research practices in English that were not followed in their prior institutions, in addition to making sure they followed sound scholarly practices throughout the semester to ensure they did so across other courses in their programs.
2. **Grading library assignments:** When it came to the assignments tasked by the librarian, students needed to be directed by the faculty

member that these assignments were part and parcel of the main course assignments. Discussions were held between the faculty member and the librarian about the importance of grading the assignments in order for them to be taken seriously by the students. The challenge of who would be grading them was settled by the librarian agreeing to allow the faculty member to do that.

3. **Unforeseen gaps:** Ideas related to research ethics proved to be unclear to the students in this course. Therefore, more time than anticipated was spent on discussing the importance of questioning the credibility of information sources in terms of plagiarism, copyright, and research ethics malpractice. Even though the concepts in the Framework covering the value and process of information creation were addressed during the first and second library instruction sessions, the concept of research ethics was not properly covered. Students continued to be hasty in trusting information posted online, and they kept assuming that they can freely use and share information without any examination of the way information was gathered, selected, and analyzed. To address this gap, we developed an unplanned learning object in the form of an infographic. The infographic, created by the library instructor and distributed in class during the third library session, included information on key principles related to research ethics such as anonymity, confidentiality, integrity, and safety of vulnerable groups. Research ethics as a concept was introduced to help students look at information and research sharing more consciously and critically.
4. **Nontransferability of skills:** Another challenge was that students did not seem to transfer all the skills acquired through the library sessions into their end-of-semester research papers. While they did well during the library sessions and successfully completed the library assignments and passed the quizzes, they seemed to have not applied all that they learned in their final paper and other course assignments. We don't think that this had anything to do with the Framework concepts, but rather it was due to the fact that students regarded the library sessions as helpful information but not core elements of the course that called for them to make significant

changes in their research habits. This required us to reexamine the process of integrating the Framework and make sure to emphasize the use of the skills learned by implementing a credit or grading system for the library components in the final paper.

5. **Time and core content restrictions:** An anticipated challenge came with providing time for the library sessions without jeopardizing the original content of the course. Both librarian and instructor had to compromise to accommodate all the new content and complement each other in providing the skills needed in a course for students weak in writing and research skills.
6. **Accommodating digital scholarship:** Another challenge was the fact that other scholarly literacies were urgently emerging as important components of graduate and undergraduate studies, such as digital, data, and media literacy, along with open access scholarship. Transferring the co-design process into another course taught by the same instructor was not very simple, the reason being that other courses taught by the same instructor had different cohorts of students and assignments that required different sets of resources, skills, and support by a full-fledged librarian partner. Another librarian with digital literacy skills and exposure to digital tools and projects was embedded in the new courses, modifying the information literacy sessions to suit the new parameters of the courses.

Ways to Move Forward

Our experience suggests ways to move forward:

1. **On an institutional level:** The co-design experience created new opportunities for cooperation between the Research and Instruction Services Department and faculty members. General sessions integrated in the communication skills program are still the majority of classes. Nevertheless, in spring 2018 the University Libraries launched the Embed a Librarian in Your Class service, which was very well-received across campus. It proved again that information literacy instruction is most appreciated when it is connected to specific teaching and research goals. Since then, the University

Libraries are moving more and more toward the subject librarian research services model. In 2018 the departments of Public Health and Social Sciences were approached to integrate information literacy as a component for graduate work of their students. Both departments have approved making attending the five-part library graduate workshop series a requirement for all graduate students. Other departments are including library instruction as part of their writing in the discipline course. Furthermore, lesson plans used for this course are being adapted to different academic majors and discussed with the departmental graduate coordinators in the hope of institutionalizing the process of teaching information literacy at the graduate and departmental levels.

The library instruction program that started as a component of the communication skills program is moving ahead to provide subject-specific library sessions; today the library is increasingly offering subject-specific and graduate-level sessions, which account for almost half of the total number of offered sessions.

2. **On the course level:** Co-designing the Writing in the Disciplines course was very successful and a good start for a fully fledged partnership and cooperation with a librarian. However, learning from the above-mentioned challenges, we can improve the process of incorporating information literacy skills in the class by providing more context for plagiarism and ensuring the use of the learned skills throughout the semester. Teaming up with other faculty in the English Department to establish the components of teaching information literacy to all English 300 sections was also seen as important. Discussions on a departmental level will also encourage other faculty to team up with librarians to implement similar co-design processes in their courses.

Conclusion

Prior to the co-design workshop and the integration of the librarian's presentations, assignments, and quizzes, the instructor had the notion that one session with a holistic approach to information literacy that could be given by any available librarian would suffice. Having delved more deeply into the ACRL Framework during the co-design workshop at AUP, the instructor saw a lot more work and equitable collaboration with the librarian as more instrumental in identifying where, how, and when to begin the process of identifying students' information literacy needs. Moreover, integrating the required sessions into an already established syllabus had to be done with a librarian who is aware of and ready to share the extra workload without adding to the already heavy workload of the faculty member and without disrupting the sequencing of the assignments and materials in the course policy. Moreover, the collaboration entailed following up on students' performance throughout the semester to revise and redesign the course in the forthcoming semester. Most importantly, the relationship established between faculty member and librarian opened up new pathways for future collaborations with other library staff who could become partners in other courses.

Notes

1. Samantha Godbey and Xan Goodman, "Co-design: Integrating Information Literacy into Your Disciplinary Course" (AMICAL workshop, American University of Paris, March 31–April 1, 2017), https://www.amicalnet.org/events/co-design-integrating-information-literacy-into-your-disciplinary-course; Association of College and Research Libraries, *Framework for Information Literacy for Higher Education* (Chicago: Association of College and Research Libraries, 2016).
2. American University of Beirut, "Overview," http://www.aub.edu.lb/AboutUs/Pages/default.aspx.
3. American University of Beirut, "Mission Statement," http://www.aub.edu.lb/AboutUs/Pages/mission.aspx.
4. QS Top Universities, "QS World University Rankings: Arab Region," https://www.topuniversities.com/university-rankings/arab-region-university-rankings/2018.
5. For more details, check the lesson plans "Getting Started with Graduate Research" and "Research in the Discipline" in this book.
6. For more details, see the lesson plans "Getting Started with Graduate Research" and "Research in the Discipline" in this book.
7. Association of College and Research Libraries, *Information Literacy Competency Standards for Higher Education* (Chicago: Association of College and Research Libraries, 2000).

Bibliography

American University of Beirut. "Mission Statement." http://www.aub.edu.lb/AboutUs/Pages/mission.aspx.

———. "Overview." http://www.aub.edu.lb/AboutUs/Pages/default.aspx.

Association of College and Research Libraries. *Framework for Information Literacy for Higher Education*. Chicago: Association of College and Research Libraries, 2016.

———. *Information Literacy Competency Standards for Higher Education*. Chicago: Association of College and Research Libraries, 2000.

Godbey, Samantha, and Xan Goodman. "Co-design: Integrating Information Literacy into Your Disciplinary Course." AMICAL workshop, American University of Paris, March 31–April 1, 2017. https://www.amicalnet.org/events/co-design-integrating-information-literacy-into-your-disciplinary-course.

QS Top Universities. "QS World University Rankings: Arab Region." https://www.topuniversities.com/university-rankings/arab-region-university-rankings/2018.

CASE STUDY 8

Co-designing and Beyond

The Evolution of the AUBG Information Literacy Program as Inspired by the ACRL Framework

Krasimir Spasov

Information Literacy Librarian, American University in Bulgaria

Background

The American University in Bulgaria (AUBG) was established in 1991 and since then has been developing steadily by improving its educational programs. AUBG is the first American-style liberal arts institution in Eastern Europe, with more than 1,000 students from over forty countries. Being able to choose from arts, humanities, business, computer science, and other fields, AUBG students build their own curricula and can declare a double major, a major and a minor, or a major and two minors.

Among the many departments at AUBG is Panitza Library, which takes great pride in the services and resources it provides. My career as a librarian began in late 2010 when I started as a circulation and reserve librarian at Panitza Library. My passion for exploring new horizons led me to graduate from a library science school in 2014 and then immediately start a new position as an information literacy (IL) librarian.

Panitza Library's IL program officially began in 1999 and has been evolving in slow, and at times insufficient, steps ever since. With the advent of the ACRL *Framework for Information Literacy for Higher Education*, it was clear that we had to make many changes to our IL program.[1] However, what was causing a bump in the start for us was the actual reading of the threshold frames. Why were there no Standards anymore?[2] What were those thresholds to pass, knowledge practices, and dispositions? Why this change from the Standards to concepts with complex intellectual applications? All these questions (and many more!) lay in front of me as an instructional librarian back in 2015. My AUBG library colleagues and I tried to brainstorm ideas on how we could incorporate these new practices into our trainings and, more importantly, how we could convince AUBG disciplinary faculty of the usefulness of these frames, as we did not fully understand them ourselves.

There came along two major training events that helped me clear the uncertainty in my mind. The first was the annual AMICAL conference and meeting held in that same year the draft frames were brought out to the general public. AUBG was the host for this conference in 2015, and the main topic was naturally the ACRL Framework. Because it was my first conference of such scope, I had the opportunity to meet a lot of IL professionals and exchange expertise with them. Through presentations, workshops, and formal and informal discussions with seminar participants, I was able to grasp the main purpose and use of these frames as well as the necessity for this change from the Standards to a Framework. To be honest, I felt relieved to learn that other colleagues from similar institutions were experiencing the same challenges as I was.

The Co-design Experience

The other training that helped me further my understanding of the ACRL frames was the co-design workshop held in April 2017.[3] The main idea of this workshop grabbed my attention instantaneously as it aimed at an opportunity for not only refreshing an existing IL program in terms of content and delivery, but also collaborating with faculty—something that I thought had been slipping through my working process. I immediately proposed this opportunity to Rositsa Gradeva, a long-term history professor at AUBG, and we submitted an application to participate in this training. This workshop seemed to be a favorable chance to develop a collaboration between a faculty member and a librarian as well as an opportunity to pursue an embedded librarianship approach to a course. I daresay that I had come with a bag full of prospective projects that seemed to me at that stage a bit unrealistic, as I did not see how they could be achieved by working with the ACRL frames. However, through the examples, explanations, and practical activities in this workshop, I started to realize that certain projects are indeed possible. The veil seemed to be lifting from the state of confusion and misunderstanding I was in about the Framework prior to the workshop.

During the workshop, it became obvious to me that among the advantages of the Framework that outweigh the Standards is that it gives freedom to the faculty member and librarian to consider different approaches for collaboration. The Framework is not a list of mandatory standards and outcomes that the librarian should follow—it is a means or a channel of connecting the library with the classroom. The Framework set the stage for our collaborative team to contemplate questions such as these:

- What basic skills on the cyclical nature of the research process should the students already possess? What assumptions do we, as experts in our fields, have about students' previous history knowledge base?
- How can we guide students toward enhancing their IL skills in the context of the history course and discipline?
- How can a threshold concept transform the way a student understands or interprets something? Can threshold concepts be so powerful as to facilitate the unlearning of previous knowledge?

Prior to the co-design workshop, Professor Gradeva and I had identified our first collaborative project: to co-teach a three-credit, 300-level history course called History 305: Topics in Southeast European History: Balkan Minorities in the International Relations, 1774–1920s. It was a writing-intensive course on Ottoman history whose biggest assignment was a term or research paper, and my role was in a way acting as the interface between the research and writing processes. This was for me a tall order as it meant that I had to be almost proficient with certain historic facts and vocabulary so that I could be an active part of the teaching process. What helped me the most with this issue was Professor Gradeva's suggestion that I take one of her other courses as a prerequisite to our co-designed course. After considering it carefully, I accepted the opportunity, and class after class I realized that was indeed an excellent idea, because this way I was able to learn about the Balkan minorities and thus prepare for a better research process that would benefit the History 305 students in their research. Undeniably, this turned out to be the first lesson I learned: in order to be able to teach effective research skills in a disciplinary context, you must first be equipped with a certain amount of knowledge on the subject matter. I still recall previous talks among colleagues at our library about the possibility of transforming our positions into subject librarians, but we never got to any such change. How I wish this could have happened much earlier! My subject expertise is related to the study and acquisition of foreign languages (English and German), so you can imagine what a great amount of new material I had to deal with for this course. This inevitably led to enormous pressure—having to teach and at the same time having to learn a completely new sphere of study in addition to performing all my other library duties.

The History 305 course included a couple of other writing tasks for the students. Besides the most important assignment—the research paper—students also had to write an essay during the midterm exam (based on the lectures in class and some research on the discussed topics) and a homework assignment. The research paper was divided into stages: the students had to draft an outline of the paper, build a preliminary bibliography, and then write the actual paper. The final stage of the paper was to give a short oral presentation about their topic. My biggest contribution to this class came in week 5 after the start of the course, when I had to give a workshop on the research process, talk about searching in the library's catalog and databases, and explain the difference between primary and secondary sources. The seminar also allotted some time for the students to perform some searching on their own to put into practice what they had learned. To me, the class was successful and engaging for the students, as the professor and I had wisely scheduled the date of the workshop in alignment with the overall course schedule. Professor Gradeva had taught all the necessary material and prepared students for what was ahead so when they came to the workshop, there were no surprises. Furthermore, the library workshop timing coincided with the due date when students had to hand in their outlines and preliminary bibliography.

Throughout this course, Professor Gradeva and I worked on several frames, namely Authority Is Constructed and Contextual, Scholarship as Conversation, Research as Inquiry, and Searching as Strategic Exploration. The professor carried the heavy load of building and imparting the knowledge about the frames to the students in the course context. While some of these overlap in their broadest sense, my largest contribution to the course was with the last-mentioned frame, Searching as Strategic Exploration. During the one-shot workshop, my aim was to introduce students to four major knowledge practices (as outlined in the ACRL Framework):

> identify interested parties, such as scholars, organizations, governments, and industries, who might produce information about a topic and then determine how to access that information
>
> ...
>
> use different types of searching language (e.g., controlled vocabulary, keywords, natural language) appropriately
>
> ...
>
> understand how information systems (i.e., collections of recorded information) are organized in order to access relevant information
>
> ...
>
> match information needs and search strategies to appropriate search tools[4]

The students' increased understanding of this concept was achieved through a demonstration and presentation of the library catalog and database as well as a facilitated discussion. This discussion explored how databases and catalogs are built, how and from where to start the research process, and how to choose the best tools and keywords when searching. The discussion gave me evidence about the level students were already at with this frame—that is, which students were novice and which ones were more advanced learners. In terms of the affective, attitudinal, or valuing dimension of the learning process—that is, the acquired dispositions—students were guided to do the following (as outlined in the ACRL Framework):

> understand that first attempts at searching do not always produce adequate results
>
> realize that information sources vary greatly in content and format and have varying relevance and value, depending on the needs and nature of the search
>
> seek guidance from experts, such as librarians, researchers, and professionals

> ...
>
> persist in the face of search challenges, and know when they have enough information to complete the information task[5]

In my view, a one-shot session would not be enough to illustrate the nature and meaning of a single frame. This single session would need to be set in the context of a specific course that is discussing these frames throughout. During the library session, I noticed that some of the students had the usual attitude of already knowing it all. They felt very confident in their research skills up until the moment they had to put into practice all they had been taught. I saw them pushing their limits to find the best relevant sources and thus question their own knowledge base and assumptions. I believe the practical exercises coupled with the discussion contributed to a shift in students' perceptions of the research process. Not only does this speak to the troublesome nature of the Framework but also to the transformative quality of these concepts. While the Standards emphasized the teaching of mere skills and abilities, the Framework expands that notion to also consider the context and reasons why these skills exist, evolve, transform, or coalesce.

Beyond the Co-designed Course

During the history course, I started considering how I could improve our IL program, having gained some experience from working collaboratively in this embedded opportunity. Since the establishment of our program, there have not been many changes introduced other than some improved library presentations and demonstrations on the databases. Moreover, our IL program as a whole put the accent on the alignment with the ACRL Standards when teaching in the rest of the courses. While this approach was still working with other professors, the need to refresh and change our program was on the horizon. The AUBG IL program had to improve its content and the skills it aimed to teach in order to reflect the new methods and trends in library instruction.

Certain talks began in spring 2017, and by fall 2018 this program had undergone changes that brought it out of its standstill. During this period, I volunteered to be an advisor in information literacy during an attempt to revamp the AUBG general education program. This helped me collect data on what should be included in or excluded from our IL program as well as establishing new connections with faculty for possible future collaborations. I was able to spread the word among other AUBG professors and kindle their interest about prospective projects. For me, the freshman writing courses are the best milieu for students' acquisition and development of IL skills. Thus, new and refreshed lessons were offered in fall 2018 as an overarching and holistic series of IL practice that aimed to introduce the ACRL frames in the two mandatory English writing classes.

The first major change was introduced in the English department, with which we collaboratively worked on creating a number of IL lesson plans. A strong emphasis was placed on the role of these lessons to disseminate knowledge for the improvement of students' critical and analytical skills in a digital environment. Information and digital literacy instruction was supported by flipping some of the content that students had to learn, do, or share as a course homework activity, and then the IL librarian would observe their progress and performance. One of the main goals of all these activities was to cultivate a research mindset among the AUBG freshmen and thus prepare them for more advanced courses (Research as Inquiry).

Overall, this series consists of a string of three one-shot sessions offered throughout one academic year. The first session is held during the freshman orientation week, when we present the library's services and resources. The aim of this lesson is to introduce the frame Information Creation as a Process and lay the foundations for reflective and conscious thinking about the different formats of information and the various channels authors use to spread it. This seems to be a difficult demand for the students, as, firstly, our students come from very diverse backgrounds and some of them have not ever visited a library in their lives, and secondly, because most do not even contemplate the different aspects of the phased process of creating and disseminating a piece of information.

For this session, students are divided into groups of no more than fifteen people and are gathered in a computer lab located near the library. Half of the lesson takes place in the lab, where students are presented mostly with the library's electronic content. We teach them basic library vocabulary as well as introductory information about types of materials. Part of the lab training also includes working with the catalog to understand its different facets, such as locations, formats, and subjects. The presentation is delivered not only through lecturing, but also through video tutorials and discussions. Then, students are taken to the actual library and instead of having the regular (and at times boring) tour, we offer them a game that ends with a small treat. The main purpose of this game is to teach students how to navigate the library and find books. It is an easy and quick game, but it helps to teach students how to read call numbers as well as getting oriented to the library's building and facilities.

The next session takes place during the English 101 (Exposition) classes, when students are learning to write mainly essays and are barely introduced to the research process. The professors decide exactly when the library training should take place after a consultation with the IL librarian. The main objective of these one-shot sessions is to introduce students to critical and analytical thinking skills. At this stage, students should be fully exposed to the frame Information Creation as a Process by talking about the actual process of creating scholarly and nonscholarly information and the means of spreading it. In addition, students are also introduced to the frame Information Has Value and more specifically to the concept of not stealing someone's ideas, thoughts, or arguments. This frame is of great significance because many students transitioning to university have a hard time breaking free from old habits such as copying and pasting information and presenting it as their own. Since this is the first time that many of them are confronted with the ethical side of using information, this frame is introduced by discussing the topic of plagiarism and how to avoid it. During the class, students are given examples of how to ethically borrow someone's ideas without being fully introduced to the various styles of citation. A more detailed overview of citations is given in the last of the three one-shot sessions.

These lessons are held in labs, as students need to have access to computers equipped with an internet connection. The session starts with a game that asks students to brainstorm ideas for keywords based on visual materials. Then the class smoothly transitions to working with texts and extracting keywords. Students are also asked to identify key terms from an essay topic and then consider alternative, broader, and narrower terms. Supplied with these examples, students then use the library catalog and databases to learn how to navigate in the catalog and use our discovery tool. After all this, students are asked to try to explain what the process of creating a piece of information would be based on the examples thus far. These exercises aim to help students understand the phases of how information is created and how to be more independent when they write. The class ends with a discussion on what plagiarism is and how to avoid it. In addition, students take a plagiarism exercise to find out whether a random student's text is a case of plagiarism or not. The difficulty in this exercise comes from the fact that these are first-semester freshman students and therefore know little to nothing about citation rules. We therefore provide them with a bibliography and introduce them to the basic in-text use of someone's ideas.

The third and final session takes place during the second semester of the first year. It is part of the English 102 class Writing Academic Research Papers. As the name suggests, here freshmen are introduced to the process of doing research and thus the frames used are Searching as Strategic Exploration and Research as Inquiry. The library class always takes place in a computer lab so that students can not only learn from the presentation and demo, but also put into practice all they have learned. The core of these workshops is to teach students how to build a bibliography based on a topic, how to improve their searching skills through developing a variety of strategies, and how to distinguish between primary, secondary, and tertiary sources (almost the same as what I did for the co-designed history class). The key element from the frame Searching as Strategic Exploration emphasized during the class is that "searching for information is often nonlinear and iterative, requiring the evaluation of a range of information sources and the mental flexibility to pursue alternate avenues as new understanding develops."[6] This is the pivot point of the workshop, and to accomplish a more comprehensive exploration of this concept during the session, most of the content is flipped. Prior to the workshop, students are asked to learn some content in the form of reading texts, watching tutorials, and completing some exercises to prepare for the actual workshop. We find this useful, as a one-shot session is not enough time to impart research skills and explore the broader concepts from the frames. Thus, student practice in the evaluation and ethical usage of information is extended through the means of additional exercises on our database.

Conclusion

Overall, the new AUBG IL program, aimed currently at the English courses, can certainly be defined as revamped thanks to the aha! moments gathered during the co-design workshop. Having been able to develop a collaborative project with the frames in mind helped me realize the true benefit of using the Framework—that is, it has indeed been created to facilitate such projects. Though the Standards did not abolish partnerships between faculty and librarians, they suggested more or less teaching on your own. Because the Framework and its core concepts are ideas that should be explored both in the classroom and throughout one's life, I learned that the Framework provides numerous opportunities for collaboration as we work to help students achieve both in-class and lifelong learning.

My other takeaway is the lessons I learned while collaborating with Professor Gradeva for the history course. I am now absolutely positive that in order to co-teach, you will have to be a good subject librarian. Undeniably, if I had to co-teach at that high a level, I would have struggled with basic knowledge needed during the research process. In addition, the library's one-shot workshop was successful and did not feel disconnected from the course thanks to the professor's guidance and prior buildup of knowledge. Another important lesson for me was to approach one frame at a time, as it is not obligatory (is impossible, I should say) to cram all in one or two library sessions!

Moving forward, the success of our IL program with the English department has also led to increased participation in the AUBG first-year experience course. Two workshops will be offered every semester to include more varied literacy knowledge in addition to IL. The primary objective is to add visual and digital literacy to broaden students' horizons and enrich the content of these courses in terms of more varied competencies. However, addressing the ACRL frames in the context of the first-year experience seems to be a multifaceted challenge. There is no writing assignment and are no research endeavors. Freshmen are introduced to the idea of being university students and are taught a number of skills to help them manage stress when overwhelmed with lots of studying. Therefore, these two one-shot classes will continue the idea of enhancing students' critical and analytical thinking skills. The main goal of these workshops will be to upgrade these competencies through the aforementioned series of one-shot sessions designed for the English writing courses.

Overall, what seemed to be an idea for an individual project expanded to a change on a program level. The co-design workshop started with a single faculty-librarian collaboration and led to a new and polished IL program at AUBG that utilizes the core ideas of the ACRL *Framework for Information Literacy for Higher Education.*

Notes

1. Association of College and Research Libraries, *Framework for Information Literacy for Higher Education* (Chicago: Association of College and Research Libraries, 2016).
2. Association of College and Research Libraries, *Information Literacy Competency Standards for Higher Education* (Chicago: Association of College and Research Libraries, 2000).
3. Samantha Godbey and Xan Goodman, "Co-design: Integrating Information Literacy into Your Disciplinary Course" (AMICAL workshop, American University of Paris, March 31–April 1, 2017), https://www.amicalnet.org/events/co-design-integrating-information-literacy-into-your-disciplinary-course.
4. Association of College and Research Libraries, *Framework*, under "Searching as Strategic Exploration: Knowledge Practices."
5. Association of College and Research Libraries, *Framework*, under "Searching as Strategic Exploration: Dispositions."
6. Association of College and Research Libraries, *Framework*, under "Searching as Strategic Exploration."

Bibliography

Association of College and Research Libraries. *Framework for Information Literacy for Higher Education*. Chicago: Association of College and Research Libraries, 2016.

———. *Information Literacy Competency Standards for Higher Education*. Chicago: Association of College and Research Libraries, 2000.

Godbey, Samantha, and Xan Goodman. "Co-design: Integrating Information Literacy into Your Disciplinary Course." AMICAL workshop, American University of Paris, March 31–April 1, 2017. https://www.amicalnet.org/events/co-design-integrating-information-literacy-into-your-disciplinary-course.

SECTION III
Lesson Plans

LESSON PLAN 1

Getting Started with Graduate Research

Fatmeh Charafeddine

Associate University Librarian, Research and Academic Collaboration Services University Libraries, American University of Beirut, Lebanon

Brief Course Description

English 300, Writing in the Disciplines, is a course designed to assist students with their graduate-level writing in English. The course begins with an introduction to academic writing in general and then moves on to doing research and writing in specific disciplines. Students are asked to work in groups of three to five to design and conduct research in their academic field. Part of the course focuses on introducing information literacy skills, including locating relevant resources, learning advanced search techniques and strategies, evaluating information, understanding copyright issues, and considering the ways scholars work collaboratively and deal with issues of intellectual property and plagiarism.

Student Level

Students taking English 300 are usually in their first semester as graduate students at the American University of Beirut (AUB). Many of them are international students from other Arab countries or from other universities in Lebanon. They have very different backgrounds in information literacy, writing skills, and doing research. Students in this class need to learn about the different types of information, where and how to find relevant information, and how to assess, select, and use information in an effective and responsible way. The number of students taking the class is twenty.

Context for the Lesson

This lesson is the first of four library instruction sessions that were integrated in the course. This lesson aims to introduce students to the different types of information and how to evaluate and use each type effectively. Students, looking for information and aiming to produce new knowledge, need to understand the process and mediums of information production and dissemination. They need to know that information has value stemming from its quality, authorship, and credibility; access to information of higher quality in most cases entails a financial fee.

Frames Addressed

All concepts in the ACRL *Framework for Information Literacy for Higher Education* could apply here,[1] but the focus will be on discussing how information comes in different mediums and is published at different times for different purposes and audiences and how information sources are protected by copyright laws and access to information in most cases is not free of charge. Thus, the frames addressed are the following:

- **Information Creation as a Process:** While graduate students need to look for relevant information regardless of information format or type, they need to understand that the way information is communicated has a great effect on how information is perceived and used.
- **Information Has Value:** This frame will help the library explain that scholarly research is costly to conduct and publish and is usually accessed through paid library subscriptions or through open access publishing protocols.

Session Learning Outcomes

- Identify the different characteristics of information according to its publishing format, purpose, and audience.
- Recognize that the author and the publisher of information determine the terms of sharing and using information.

Estimated Total Time Required

1½ hours

Venue

Classroom in the English department

Materials Needed

- Laptop for the PowerPoint presentation
- Learning materials to share for class activities: journal article, magazine article, newspaper article, report by a consulting agency, book, government document, photo, and blog post on the topic of waste management. Materials are published on different dates.

Learning Activities

1. **Start with pre-session question and discussion (30 minutes)**
   - Pose three questions to the class:
     - How do you usually choose your research topic?
     - Where do you look for information?
     - How do you assess the information you found?
   - Select students who wish to answer the questions and open the discussion for each answer. Make sure that students recognize that the library is the best place to start their research, to find answers, and to search for all types of resources. Help students come to the conclusion that scholarly research has moral and financial value.

2. **PowerPoint presentation (30 minutes)**

   The presentation covers the different categories and formats of information publishing with a focus on materials most relevant to graduate research. The library web page is used to walk students through the different types of resources available to them: for example, books, articles, encyclopedias, newspapers, dissertations, audiovisual materials, and special collections. Characteristics and academic use of each type of information are explained. A conversation is then opened, and students are asked to identify the type of resource they would use when looking for background information, facts and evidence, research findings, analysis, data, news, and editorials. The class instructor can interject here to make the question and answers more relevant to the class assignment or research projects. The librarian uses the conversation to lead to the categorization of information into primary, secondary, and tertiary sources. The role of primary resources in graduate research is highlighted as an important component to clarify possible misconceptions and provide evidence coming from original sources and firsthand information and materials. The Library Archives and Special Collections web page is then introduced; quick links to the collections, finding aids, and search tools are demonstrated.

The presentation then moves to information ownership and value, another important concept related to information use in research. The process of information production is discussed, and the roles of the author, editor, and publisher are described. The exclusive right to determine the terms of sharing and using information is clarified, and information on copyright laws is shared. Then the financial cost of information production is described as an important element that is usually misleadingly overlooked; the example of the cost of library subscribed resources is used to show that information has ownership rights and financial cost. As responsible researchers, graduate students are advised to evaluate information critically and to use information responsibly, giving credit to authors and respecting copyright terms.

3. Class activities, hands-on exercise (30 minutes)

- Students are divided into groups of three to five working on the same research project for the class. Learning materials on waste management are handed out to the groups, one type of material for each group (article, book, news, etc.). Students are asked to examine the material assigned to their group and report on its relevance to a research project. (10 minutes)

- A student from each group reports to the class on the potential use of the sample research material that was assigned to the group. (10 minutes)
- The class discusses the use of each material type, including information freely available on the internet and information from different date ranges. (10 minutes)
- The instructor and the librarian take notes to include in the final course assessment report.[2]

4. Assessment: Take-home quiz

Assessment happens as observation by the librarian and instructor during the class activities and through a take-home quiz:

- Use the library webpage to locate different types of resources for your research topic, (e.g., books, news, scholarly articles, etc.). Bring a list of your findings to the next class.
- Find one article in Wikipedia about your topic.
- Explain briefly how you are going to use each source to support your research paper.
- Find and scan the bibliography in one or more of the located resources and demonstrate how research is usually documented in order to give evidence and credibility.

The quiz is discussed in the next session as a learning activity and is handed in to the class instructor for assessment.

Notes

1. Association of College and Research Libraries, *Framework for Information Literacy for Higher Education* (Chicago: Association of College and Research Libraries, 2016).
2. For the final course assessment report, see also the case study "Redesigning a Writing-Intensive Graduate Course: An Information Literacy Case Study at AUB" in this book.

Bibliography

Association of College and Research Libraries. *Framework for Information Literacy for Higher Education*. Chicago: Association of College and Research Libraries, 2016.

Identifying Information Sources

Tatev Zargaryan

Library Systems and E-services Librarian, American University of Armenia

Brief Course Description

Expository Writing is designed to develop students' writing skills for use in a wide array of academic and professional contexts. Students will become familiar with the linguistic and rhetorical features of different genres of objective and informational writing, critically analyzing samples of effective writing in order to use them as models for their own work. In addition to their writing, students will develop familiarity with the library's collection of national statistical data, as well as primary sources from multilateral agencies.

Student Level

This session is taught to both freshman and sophomore students from different disciplines. The majority of students are Armenian with no prior exposure to information literacy instruction.

Context for the Lesson

For this session, students already have basic knowledge about library databases and resources, including a general understanding of using Wikipedia and search engines such as Google to find reliable information.

This session was previously taught to sophomore students in the context of an expository writing course in the fall 2017 semester. In their freshman year, the students are introduced to the mandatory information literacy session Acknowledging Sources, an introductory session that covers the basics about library resources, databases, citation styles, and paraphrasing.

The session Identifying Information Sources is especially designed as a continuation of the first session for students who are in their second year of study.

Frame Addressed

Authority Is Constructed and Contextual

Session Learning Outcomes

- Students will be able to differentiate between peer-reviewed and non-peer-reviewed sources.
- Students will learn that different sources of expertise may be needed for different types of information needs.

Estimated Total Time Required

This session requires a maximum of 45 minutes of class time to present the content and lead the in-class activity.

Materials Needed

- Two or more different types of sources among the following:
  - peer-reviewed article
  - Wikipedia article
  - current online news
  - biased op-ed
- Identifying Information Sources Matrix handout (see appendix LP2A)
- Computer
- Projector screen
- PowerPoint presentation about types of information
- Pens

Learning Activities

The session is divided in two parts to give the students the opportunity to understand the concepts discussed and to reflect on the reliability of the sources.

1. In the **first segment of the session**, which lasts approximately 15–20 minutes, the librarian will introduce the following topics:
   - What are information, types of formats, and types of sources?
     - information needs (casual and academic) and research priorities (background knowledge, current information, deep scholarship, persuasion)
     - critical evaluation of information based on criteria such as authority, currency, bias, and quality
2. The **second segment of the session** includes the in-class activity Identifying Information Sources. The activity is designed to last 15 minutes. The librarian distributes sources that the students read and evaluate by using the handout Identifying Information Sources Matrix. This exercise ensures that students really understand the importance of interpreting their academic needs when they can use different types of sources and what information they should consider reliable. The librarian can use a Think-Pair-Share classroom strategy to initiate an active discussion during the in-class activity.

The session ends with a question-and-answer session to answer remaining questions.

Assessment

The librarian assesses student learning by analyzing the responses to the Identifying Information Sources Matrix.

The class discussion gives further insights into how students evaluate the reliability of sources.

APPENDIX LP2A

Identifying Information Sources Matrix

Read the texts provided, paying special attention to the quality of the sources of information. Then compare the quality of these sources by filling in the chart below.

	Source 1	Source 2	Source 3	Source 4
Who is the author of this article?				
Where did this article come from? (be as specific as possible)				
What is this article's date of publication?				
Which article best provides: • Background knowledge • Current information • Deep scholarship • Persuasion				
On a scale of 1 (lowest) to 4 (highest), rank this source's quality and reliability.				

Exploring Creativity, Innovation, and Invention

Jorge F. Sosa
University Librarian, American University of Paris, France

The following lesson plan should not be considered without having read the contexts of the American University of Paris's first-year course called FirstBridge, as explained by the author in the case study "*Amalia y Yo*."

Brief Course Description

This lesson plan has been applied in the context of a FirstBridge at The American University of Paris (AUP). The name of the FirstBridge is Create: Ways of World Making. A FirstBridge is composed of two classes taught by two different professors, teaching different disciplines with a transversal topic that bridges both. In the fall of 2017, the FirstBridge Create: Ways of World Making integrated the classes Art and Science of Creating Digital Stuff and Studio Class. The FirstBridge includes weekly reflective seminars with the two faculty members, and some of these seminars are devoted to information literacy for both courses together.

Student Level

All students enrolled in FirstBridge are in their first semester. AUP has a very international group of students with very diverse educational backgrounds and therefore very different levels of information literacy.

Main Topics of the Class Session

- Search for information
- Search for scholarly information
- Analysis of web sources
- Criteria for analysis of web sources
- The deep web
- Critical thinking
- Awareness techniques of fake news

Context for the Lesson

During this reflective seminar, the two disciplinary faculty and the librarian meet with the same group of students several times during the semester. As it is a reflective seminar, it is important to flip the classroom and allow for more group student learning.

The librarian and the two faculty teach with the ACRL *Framework for Information Literacy for Higher Education* in mind, mostly dealing with the frames Scholarship as a Conversation and Information Creation as a Process.[1]

The librarian must figure out how the information literacy concepts will integrate with the central disciplinary concepts of both FirstBridge classes, which in this particular case are creativity, innovation, and invention.

Before the first reflective seminar, the two faculty members and the librarian took the students to the 2017 Paris *Off du Design* exhibit, where creation, invention, and innovation are illustrated.

The students do not need to do any preparatory work prior to this reflective seminar.

While this lesson plan was designed for this specific course, it can be modified to fit other design courses, especially those with long class sessions.

Frames Addressed

- Information Creation as a Process
- Scholarship as a Conversation

Session Learning Outcomes

Some of the learning outcomes presented below belong to the two courses' learning outcomes. They are intended to give some context; they overarch the classes of both faculty members and the information literacy activities. It is important to say that this lesson plan will not attempt to assess all those overarching learning objectives, but only some of them.

Our students will understand that

- information systems are organized and complex
- there are positive and negative aspects of information found on the web
- there is a difference between the information available on the web and on the deep web
- they should start using criteria of web evaluation (AUPAC criteria[2])
- academic research's raison d'être is to acquire new information, answer questions, resolve problems, and generate new ideas
- scholars are creators of information and that there is something called peer-reviewed information

Our students will be able to

- apply the AUPAC criteria when they are in front of a web source or a database article
- identify sources providing scholarly information and differentiate with the pragmatic or utilitarian source of information

Our students will value

- the variety of types of information resources they have at their fingertips
- the fact that the library can be a key contributor to their academic success[3]

Estimated Total Time Required

2 hours and 40 minutes (two class periods of 1 hour and 20 minutes each, with a short 5–8-minute pause in between)

Venue

Library research room

Materials Needed

Ideally, this lesson will happen in a smart classroom or a computer lab equipped with a computer (with PowerPoint and internet access) connected to a projector and screen, a laser pointer, and a whiteboard.

Students need to have access to computers to do the pre-assessment and later to do the web evaluation exercises.

This lesson also requires online reference resources (e.g., Credo Reference, Gale Virtual Reference Library, Oxford Reference Online).

Learning Activities

1. In the first activity, the students take the information literacy pre-assessment in order to establish their level of information literacy and their familiarity with libraries and library services. This instrument will serve later in the semester to measure student progress when the results are compared with those from a post-assessment administered after the last reflective seminar with the librarian. (estimated time: 20 minutes)
2. The librarians inform the students about two important rules during the reflective seminars:
   - The reflective seminar requires personal investment and participation.
   - Because they come from very different backgrounds, *there are no stupid questions*, as they are in the classroom to learn.
3. The next step is to have students explain in their own words their personal notions of creativity, innovation, and invention and contrast these definitions. (estimated time: 5–8 minutes)
   After the open discussion, where imprecise personal notions contrast and sometimes even clash, we try to define boundaries between each notion. Both faculty members present during the reflective seminar help in discussing the concepts by applying them to both of their disciplines.
   If questions remain unanswered, the librarian points the students to

the library online reference resources, such as Credo Reference, Gale Virtual Reference Library and Oxford Reference Online. This will help the students to look up, evaluate, and agree on the definition the group selects as the best for the class. It is important that students realize where the definition comes from.

4. The librarian presents a short twenty-slide PowerPoint presentation on evaluating web sources.[4] The presentation touches things such as the richness and complexity of the web sources, the importance of understanding URLs, the instability of sources, Google as a business, the internet not being a neutral arena, the possibility of bias, the web versus the deep web, scholarship, and authority—contextual and as a construction. The presentation also presents the five criteria of web evaluation: authority, updates, purpose, access, and content. After the presentation, the librarian hands out a printout of the five criteria.
5. This group activity involves analyzing websites and reporting back to the class to compare and compete against the other groups in the class.
   The librarian divides the class in groups of three students. Each group looks at a website and critically applies the five criteria of web evaluation.
   A key element of this activity is that each website should be analyzed by two separate groups. The pool of websites should be purposely a mixture of sites, such as a website related to Le Corbusier, a website related to a contemporary French designer that the group was able to see at the 2017 *Off du Design* exhibit, and other general selected spoof websites.
   The groups that analyzed the same website present their findings according to the web evaluation criteria, and then they discuss, compare, and contrast their analyses. In turn, all groups present in front of the rest of the class. This can become a very rich and dynamic activity that should motivate active learning.
   Since the students had the opportunity to see concrete examples of creativity, invention, and innovation during the *Off du Design de Paris*, they also analyzed the assigned web sources in terms of

authority, relevance, updates, purpose, biases, and so on, and they could see how information and object creation are part of the individual's creative process. Finally, they compared their findings with scholarly sources.

6. This activity is the wrap-up. Apply the classroom assessment technique of the Muddiest Point to assess what the most challenging part of the content was and to allow students with possible challenges to better understand or to pose additional questions.[5] On the following information literacy session, the points of the Muddiest Point should be part of a recap.

Assessment

The method of assessment used is AUP's pre- and post-assessment to measure the progress made by the students from the beginning of the FirstBridge to the very last reflective seminar session, during which the students take the post-assessment. Both pre- and post-assessments mirror each other in the type of questions asked, and in the past they incorporated the ACRL Standards.[6] Now AUP librarians are in the process of testing these assessments to integrate the ACRL Framework instead.

In addition to the pre- and post-assessment, we conduct short and easy individual session assessments as needed, such as the classroom assessment technique of the Muddiest Point.[7] Assessment also occurs informally during class discussion when the two faculty members observe student progress.

Finally, faculty can observe progress in the final student projects. Given the context of FirstBridge, the librarians cannot add more activities to the already-rich FirstBridge.

Notes

1. Association of College and Research Libraries, *Framework for Information Literacy for Higher Education* (Chicago: Association of College and Research Libraries, 2016).
2. The AUPAC web analysis criteria are authority, updates, purpose, access, and content.
3. Criteria adapted from Steely Library, "Information Literacy Framework Outcomes," July 9, 2015, https://docs.google.com/

document/d/1KnPAvzqNDVUBB0eveF3kMAU6udRQV0v8PTEEZ0_51OU/edit?pref=2&pli=1.

4. In the case of this first-year experience, it would probably be more logical to continue discussing the online resources, but since students often go first to Google, the faculty members and the librarian decided to deal with web evaluation from the very start and address the library online resources in the reflective seminars to come.
5. As described in Thomas A. Angelo and K. Patricia Cross, *Classroom Assessment Techniques*, 2nd ed. (San Francisco: Jossey-Bass, 1993), 154–58.
6. Association of College and Research Libraries, *Information Literacy Competency Standards for Higher Education* (Chicago: Association of College and Research Libraries, 2000).
7. Angelo and Cross, *Classroom Assessment Techniques*, 154–58.

Bibliography

Angelo, Thomas A., and K. Patricia Cross. *Classroom Assessment Techniques: A Handbook for College Teachers*, 2nd ed. San Francisco: Jossey-Bass, 1993.

Association of College and Research Libraries. *Framework for Information Literacy for Higher Education*. Chicago: Association of College and Research Libraries, 2016.

———. *Information Literacy Competency Standards for Higher Education*. Chicago: Association of College and Research Libraries, 2000.

Steely Library. "Information Literacy Framework Outcomes." July 9, 2015. https://docs.google.com/document/d/1KnPAvzqNDVUBB0eveF3kMAU6udRQV0v8PTEEZ0_51OU/edit?pref=2&pli=1.

Evaluating News through the Exploration of Bias

Livia Piotto

Reference and Instruction Coordinator, Frohring Library, John Cabot University, Rome, Italy

Brief Course Description

Writing across the Media (COM 221) is a core required course for all students majoring in communications at John Cabot University (JCU). It is a writing-intensive course that exposes students to different writing techniques for a variety of formats used in the media professions and in digital multimedia production. The course aims to prepare the students for careers in the media while, at the same time, they gain practical skills that combine researching and writing.

The course is structured in four different modules, each of which builds up to an individual assignment that exposes the students to a specific writing mode.[1] Each module, and consequently each assignment, offered the possibility of integrating information literacy components that would have addressed specific research skills the students could incorporate in their writing projects.

Student Level

The course is intended for freshmen and sophomores majoring in communications. Given that John Cabot University has a varied student body that includes both resident degree-seeking students and study-abroad students (mostly from the US), there might be older students from different disciplines attending the course, but for the most part this is a course with a predominance of freshman and sophomore degree-seeking students.

Context for the Lesson

This lesson plan has been developed for the first module of COM 221. The module's final assignment is the news curation blog, for which the students choose a controversial topic or event and write five blog posts related to it. The lesson takes place toward the beginning of the module, and no preparatory work needs to be done by the students, who are at the initial stage of their research.

This lesson plan introduces students to concepts such as bias and dissemination of news to help them understand that news curation requires extensive research and analytical skills to identify how the publishing media outlets and the authors and journalists might have biases that impact the reception and understanding of news.

Frame Addressed

Authority Is Constructed and Contextual

Session Learning Outcomes

At the end of the session students will be able to

- identify how news is produced and disseminated in order to recognize the impact of bias
- examine the content of a variety of sources in order to identify how a controversial issue is treated
- discriminate between reliable and unreliable information, regardless of where it comes from, in order to share credible information

Estimated Total Time Required

75 minutes

Materials Needed

- Computers or tablets with internet access for student use (At JCU we have a mobile lab equipped with tablets, but we often rely on a BYOD practice, which is fairly easy to do, especially with communications students who are used to working on their own devices.)
- Instructor computer and projector
- Online polling tool to use for an icebreaker (for example, Poll Everywhere [https://www.polleverywhere.com/] or AnswerGarden [https://answer-garden.ch/]; Padlet [https://padlet.com/] could work as well.)
- Presentation containing different types of biases
- Link to Media Bias Chart (https://www.adfontesmedia.com/intro-to-the-media-bias-chart/) and to the blank version (https://www.adfontesmedia.com/wp-content/uploads/2017/08/Second-Edition-Blank.pdf)
- Index cards with news media organization logos and sticky tape
- Evaluating Controversial News Activity worksheets
- Subscription database for news sources

Learning Activities

1. Introduction to the session and Think-Pair-Share
   - The session begins with the librarian describing the learning outcomes and overviewing the course LibGuide.[2]
   - The librarian invites the students to start a discussion about news sources and strategies to evaluate them:
     - Where do you usually get your news from?
     - How do you decide if the information you find is trustworthy?

     The two questions are projected on the screen while the students use their devices to provide their answers via AnswerGarden.[3] Students respond as many times as they want, and after a couple of minutes, the librarian invites the students to discuss the responses as a group.

   This activity is used as an icebreaker to set the stage for the main activities of the session.

2. Direct instruction
   Following the initial guided discussion, the librarian projects a short presentation showing definitions of various cognitive bias types (specifically confirmation bias, echo chamber effect, and systematic bias) to help the students understand that biases have an impact on how news is distributed by media organizations and received by the audience. Students in this course generally come with an understanding of author bias; this direct instruction and the following activity help students to understand different layers of bias beyond author bias.

3. Media bias activity[4]
   - On the screen, the librarian projects the blank Media Bias Chart,[5] which allows students to place media sources on a chart with quality plotted against political bias. After the librarian explains how to read the chart, each student receives an index card with a media organization logo. Then the librarian asks the students to start researching the assigned media organization in order to discover useful details about the organization itself and to determine in which section of the chart they would place it based on their findings.
   - When the students finish their research (they should not be not directed to any specific research tool, but allowed to use their skills freely to analyze the media organizations), they are asked to stick the logo on the chart.
   - On the projector, the librarian switches browser tabs and projects the complete Media Bias Chart[6] to compare the original with the research conducted by the students.
   - The activity ends with a discussion of the results. The students are encouraged to share the search strategies that they used to take their final decisions.

   This activity connects back with the frame Authority Is Constructed and Contextual because it teaches students to acknowledge bias in all its forms and layers and persuades them to become aware of their own biases as well as of author and media organization biases.

Recognizing that how information is perceived is an individual construct based on the existence and subsequent acknowledgement of bias helps the students maintain an open mind toward the concept of authority.

4. Evaluating controversial news activity
   - The librarian introduces this segment of the session by briefly discussing the dangers of misleading news and pointing out that there are tools that can help readers identify fake news and verify news stories in general. Links to fact-checking websites that can be used while doing research are presented to the students. (All the resources mentioned are available on the Moodle page for the course and on the course LibGuide.)
   - After a short demo of the news database (i.e., LexisNexis), the librarian points out that critically researching news is more complicated than students normally expect and that a subscription database might help in filtering good versus bad news sources.
   - The librarian distributes the Evaluating Controversial News Activity worksheet and asks the students to complete it during their independent practice. The worksheet consists of the following instructions:
     - Search for an article that you may want to use as a source for your posts about a current, possibly controversial topic.
     - Write down the title of the article and the URL (if possible).
     - Briefly list the criteria that you use to evaluate if a piece of news is good.
     - Use fact-checking websites to analyze your source. How would you judge the piece of news?
   - This is a practice activity that is followed by a similar homework assignment in which the students have to independently research and evaluate news. Therefore the librarian collects the worksheets at the end of the activity for observational assessment, explaining

that the worksheets are not graded nor returned to the students unless they request it.

This activity is mainly aimed at encouraging students to take a skeptical perspective toward how authority is presented and to critically assess the content they encounter in their research.

5. Closing
   After collecting the worksheets, the librarian closes the session asking the students if any questions remain unanswered.

Assessment

In-class formative assessment happens at the end of the first two activities:

- A preconception check occurs in the form of the icebreaker questions that serve to prompt the discussion and to encourage "reflective metacognition"[7] about what students already know and how their knowledge can be corrected or confirmed.
- The Media Bias Chart also provides assessment of the work conducted by the students during their research. The discussion following the activity serves to clarify concepts related to bias in media organizations and to emphasize the importance of analytical news research.

Observational assessment is used to assess level 2 (Learning) of the Kirkpatrick Model.[8] This assessment method, used to look for patterns of performance across the students and to analyze student engagement, is conducted utilizing the success matrix for the activity of evaluating controversial news.[9] The assessment aims to analyze whether the students complete the worksheet, understand the importance of developing a set of criteria to analyze bias, and develop strategies to verify the trustworthiness of news sources. Success is measured quantitatively as following:

- Success: More than 75 percent of the students filled in the worksheet as requested.
- Partial success (with ample margin for improvement): 50 to 75 percent of the students filled in the worksheet as requested.
- Little success: Less than 50 percent of the students filled in the worksheet as requested.[10]

Notes

1. For a full description of the four different modules, see also the case study titled "Integrating Information Literacy in a Communication Writing Course" and the second library session's lesson plan from the same course titled "What's behind That? Facts and Statistics Supporting Public Service Announcements."
2. The course guide is a sub-page of the general Communications LibGuide developed for the major. The guide is available at https://johncabot.libguides.com/communications/COM221, and it includes resources and activities used in the library sessions.
3. AnswerGarden was chosen because it is an easy-to-use tool that can elicit brief answers that are automatically displayed in a word cloud that highlights recurring concepts. It is a great tool to activate student engagement.
4. This activity was adapted from the lesson plan by Darcy Gervasio, "'Pin the Source on the Spectrum': Fake News Is on a Continuum," ACRL Framework for Information Literacy Sandbox, May 12, 2017, http://sandbox.acrl.org/library-collection/pin-source-spectrum-fake-news-continuum.
5. Vanessa Otero, "Blank Media Bias Chart," 2nd ed., Ad Fontes Media, August 2017, https://www.adfontesmedia.com/wp-content/uploads/2017/08/Second-Edition-Blank.pdf.
6. Vanessa Otero, "The Media Bias Chart," version 5.1, Ad Fontes Media, https://www.adfontesmedia.com/intro-to-the-media-bias-chart.
7. Melissa Bowles-Terry and Cassandra Kvenild, *Classroom Assessment Techniques for Librarians* (Chicago: Association of College and Research Libraries, 2015), 7–11.
8. Donald L. Kirkpatrick and James D. Kirkpatrick, *Evaluating Training Programs*, 3rd ed. (San Francisco: Berrett-Koehler, 2006), http://www.aspresolver.com/aspresolver.asp?BIZP;2341903.
9. The success matrix was developed using an example included in Candice Benjes-Small et al., "Teaching Web Evaluation: A Cognitive Development Approach," *Communications in Information Literacy* 7, no. 1 (2013): 46, https://doi.org/10.15760/comminfolit.2013.7.1.133.
10. An example of the success matrix is available as a table in the lesson plan "What's behind That? Facts and Statistics Supporting Public Service Announcements."

Bibliography

Benjes-Small, Candice, Alyssa Archer, Katelyn Tucker, Lisa Vassady, and Jennifer Resor Whicker. "Teaching Web Evaluation: A Cognitive Development Approach." *Communications in Information Literacy* 7, no. 1 (2013): 39–49. https://doi.org/10.15760/comminfolit.2013.7.1.133.

Bowles-Terry, Melissa, and Cassandra Kvenild. *Classroom Assessment Techniques for Librarians*. Chicago: Association of College and Research Libraries, 2015.

Gervasio, Darcy. "'Pin the Source on the Spectrum': Fake News Is on a Continuum." ACRL Framework for Information Literacy Sandbox, May 12, 2017. http://sandbox.acrl.org/library-collection/pin-source-spectrum-fake-news-continuum.

Kirkpatrick, Donald L., and James D. Kirkpatrick. *Evaluating Training Programs: The Four Levels*, 3rd ed. San Francisco: Berrett-Koehler, 2006. http://www.aspresolver.com/aspresolver.asp?BIZP;2341903.

Otero, Vanessa. "Blank Media Bias Chart," 2nd ed. Ad Fontes Media, August 2017. https://www.adfontesmedia.com/wp-content/uploads/2017/08/Second-Edition-Blank.pdf.

———. "The Media Bias Chart," version 5.1. Ad Fontes Media. https://www.adfontesmedia.com/intro-to-the-media-bias-chart.

LESSON PLAN 5

The Beauty of Research

Michael Stöpel

User Services Librarian, American University of Paris, France

Brief Course Description

Marketing in a Global Environment is a practical hands-on introduction to marketing principles. Students learn to bring a product or service into the French and European marketplace after analyzing a need or void in the market. Students can demonstrate their understanding of the textbook by simulating a real-life project and developing a marketing plan. (Working with a real company, such as the start-up mentioned in our case study, "Developing Marketing Plans and the Beauty of Research," would be the ideal case.) The course examines marketing from a strategic and functional point of view through lectures, market research, case studies, and written analysis of the students' product or service.

Assignment

Students present their group marketing plans three times during the semester. The content of the marketing plans covers the textbook chapters as the semester advances.

Student Level

Most of the students are junior or senior students coming from different academic disciplines. In the summer, some visiting students take this course. Most students had an introduction to library resources during the first-year seminar.

Context for the Lesson

This library session is given when students start creating and researching their group presentations and a marketing plan for a product or service to bring to market. The library session takes place at the point of need, two to three weeks before the first presentations. Students are asked to find sources, typically statistics, in order to support their arguments in their marketing plan presentations and strategies. They are asked to analyze the sources and to demonstrate their quality.

This class session is co-taught by a faculty member and a librarian. The librarian takes the lead in the session, but both professor and librarian speak and interact with students.

Later during the semester, students will have to develop a survey in order to collect data about their target market.

Frames Addressed

- Information Creation as a Process
- Authority Is Constructed and Contextual

Session Learning Outcomes

Information Creation as a Process

- Students will be able to articulate the capabilities and constraints of information developed through various creation processes (knowledge practice).
- Students will be able to seek out characteristics of information products that indicate the underlying creation process (disposition).

Authority Is Constructed and Contextual

- Students will be able to use research tools and indicators of authority to determine the credibility of sources, understanding the elements that might temper this credibility (knowledge practice).
- Students will be able to use academic resources such as databases in order to find credible sources that support their argument (knowledge practice).
- Students will be able to evaluate sources in order to select them for their class presentation.

Estimated Total Time Required

80 minutes (At American University of Paris, class sessions last 1 hour and 20 minutes.)

Materials Needed

- Printed survey (ten closed questions)
  - Survey is handed out at the beginning of the library session in order to help instructors get to know students. It includes questions on student perceptions and confidence level.[1]
  - In addition to questions on whether they had a library session in the past and which search tools they tend to use, questions include the following:
    - On a scale of 5, how confident do you feel about doing research for your project?
    - Do you think that you will be able to find reliable statistics via Google for your project in this course?
    - Have you already collaborated with other students on Google documents (slides, forms) in the past?
- Computers to complete an online survey and perform research activity
- Access to a statistics database (i.e., Statista)
- Projector in classroom
- Whiteboard and whiteboard markers

Learning Activities

1. Introduction
   - saying hello
   - sharing learning outcomes
   - presenting outline of session and activities
2. Activate: Conduct survey and Think-Pair-Share. Define and discuss a selection of terms relevant to Information Creation as a Process such as

  - response rate
  - sample and sampling
  - missing data
  - socially expected replies
  - wording of questions and bias
  - funding of survey
  - bias of institution conducting the survey
  - importance of demographics

3. Showcase a statistics database (i.e., Statista).

   - application of discussed material about critical thinking about information creation (see above)
   - highlighting of the database citation tool, download feature of full text, and e-mail option

4. Meta-moment: Think-Share: one-minute paper

   - Ask students to reflect on their activities following John Dewey's idea that we learn by reflecting on experiences.
   - Two questions: What have we done so far today? Why do the learning activities matter for your group presentations?

5. Research lab

   - Group members research relevant information in light of their upcoming presentations, collecting quality resources and citations directly into their group presentation slides (i.e., using Google Slides or Office 365).
   - Instructors circulate in class to give direct feedback on sources used and students' projects.

     - Librarian focuses on in-text citations, image citations, quality of sources, and bibliography.
     - Faculty member focuses on marketing plan idea and how sources support argument.

   - It is important that the library session is scheduled not too far in advance of the group presentations of the marketing plans (at a time sometimes referred to as the teachable moment—the

moment when learning is effective because students pay attention to the learning material).
- The research lab brings together the different learning outcomes. Students apply what they have learned in light of their project.

6. Exit activity: Ask students to share their group presentation slides by e-mail with instructors for online feedback and to allow instructors to prepare the next library session.

Assessment

- Survey results in order to assess students' perceptions and confidence levels
- Online formative assessment: Looking at students' group presentation slides (i.e., Google Slides or Office 365 PowerPoint slides) in order to check their presentations and to give direct feedback, comments, and suggestions. Especially, looking at in-text citations, quality of sources, and MLA style in their shared slides.

Note

1. Melissa Bowles-Terry and Cassandra Kvenild, *Classroom Assessment Techniques for Librarians* (Chicago: Association of College and Research Libraries, 2015), 8–12.

Bibliography

Bowles-Terry, Melissa, and Cassandra Kvenild. *Classroom Assessment Techniques for Librarians.* Chicago: Association of College and Research Libraries, 2015.

You Are the Jury

Michael Stöpel

User Services Librarian, American University of Paris, France

Brief Course Description

Marketing in a Global Environment is a practical hands-on introduction to marketing principles. Students learn to bring a product or service into the French and European marketplace after analyzing a need or void in the market. Students can demonstrate their understanding of the textbook by simulating a real-life project and developing a marketing plan. (Working with a real company, such as a start-up mentioned in our impact story, would be the ideal case.) The course examines marketing from a strategic and functional point of view through lectures, market research, case studies, and written analysis of the students' product or service.

Assignment

Students present their group marketing plans three times during the semester. The content of the marketing plans covers the textbook chapters as the semester advances.

Student Level

Most of the students are junior or senior students coming from different academic disciplines. In the summer, some visiting students take this course. Most students had an introduction to library resources during the first-year seminar.

Context of the Lesson

This is the second of two library sessions, which can occur in consecutive classes, or the second session can occur later during the semester. The session aims at identifying in-text citations and image citations, evaluating the bibliography, and using and valuing sources for the presentation. Students will be asked to find sources of quality, typically statistics, in order to support their arguments in the marketing plan strategy. They will be asked to analyze the sources and to demonstrate their quality.

This class session is co-taught by a faculty member and a librarian. The librarian takes the lead of the session, but both professor and librarian speak and interact with students.

Frames Addressed

- Information Creation as a Process
- Authority Is Constructed and Contextual

Session Learning Outcomes

Information Creation as a Process

- Students will be able to articulate the capabilities and constraints of information developed through various creation processes (knowledge practice).
- Students will be inclined to seek out characteristics of information products that indicate the underlying creation process (disposition).

Authority Is Constructed and Contextual

- Students will be able to use research tools and indicators of authority to determine the credibility of sources, understanding the elements that might temper this credibility (knowledge practice).
- Students will be able to use academic resources such as databases in order to find credible sources that support their argument (knowledge practice).
- Students will be able to evaluate sources in order to select them for their class presentation.

Estimated Total Time Required

80 minutes (At American University of Paris, class sessions last 1 hour and 20 minutes.)

Materials Needed

- Marketing plan presentation done by students for the same class of a previous semester
- Presentation rubric entitled "You Are the Jury," which includes questions about being aesthetically pleasing, in-text citations, images citations, quality of sources, and the bibliography
- Librarian's slides that include correct in-text citations and a bibliography with quality sources
- SurveyMonkey or equivalent survey tool to show user survey results

Learning Activities

1. Introduction
   - saying hello
   - sharing learning outcomes
   - presenting outline of session and activities
2. Link to first session or previous session—student survey
   - Present survey results to students.
   - Discuss results briefly.
   - Reflect about learning experience (taking the survey) during the previous session—answer questions about samples and sampling, response rate, representation, missing data (missing or absent students in sample).
3. Activate: Use rubric to evaluate student presentations from a previous semester:
   - Hand out presentation rubric and explain it.
   - Think-Pair-Share

- o Silent exercise: Show two students' presentations and ask students to fill in the rubric categories.
- o Share and discuss the student answers (i.e., Start with questions such as Which of the two presentations did you prefer? Why?).
- o Ask about in-text citations, image use and citations, quality of sources, and bibliography.
- o Application of discussed material: Identify sources and statistics and apply critical questions about how information is created (i.e., response rate, sample and sampling, missing data, transparency of how statistic is produced).

4. Showcase librarian's slides. Slides include
   - correct in-text citations
   - a selected in-text citation (that is for a quality source vs. in-text citation of a less credible source)
   - an image citation
   - bibliography with quality sources

5. Meta-moment. Think/Share: one-minute paper
   - Ask students to reflect on their activities following John Dewey's idea that we learn by reflecting on experiences.
   - Why do the learning activities matter for your group presentations?

6. Research lab
   - Groups co-search and find relevant information in light of their upcoming presentations.
   - Students add quality sources to the bibliography.
   - Instructors circulate in class to give direct feedback on sources used and students' projects.
     - o Librarian focuses on in-text citations, image citations, quality of sources, bibliography.
     - o Faculty member focuses on marketing plan idea and how sources support argument in the students' presentations.

7. Exit activity. Students share slides by e-mail with instructors for online feedback.

Assessment

Online formative assessment. Looking at students' group presentation slides (i.e., Google Slides or Office 365 PowerPoint slides) in order to be able to check their presentations and to give direct feedback, comments, and suggestions. Especially looking at in-text citations, quality of sources, MLA style in their shared slides.

LESSON PLAN 7

Fear Not the Oral Communication Courses

Information Literacy in a Less Traditional Context

Ivana Stevanović

Institutional Librarian, RIT Kosovo (A.U.K), Kosovo

Brief Course Description

"This course is designed to develop oral communication skills of students through the delivering of speeches, participating in group activities, completing assigned readings, and by writing brief critiques. This public speaking course provides a basis for understanding the discipline of communication and applying principles of communication to real-world experiences."[1]

Student Level

This course is focused mostly on freshmen.

Context for the Lesson

Before and after the in-class library instruction session, students are required to watch a set of information literacy tutorials and submit a test after each of them. The time line for watching tutorials is closely connected to the course lessons that are delivered in each of the weeks. The schedule is also carefully planned so that by the time students need to work on their public speech outlines, the major information literacy topics related to the research process have been covered.

Frames Addressed

- Information Creation as a Process
- Authority Is Constructed and Contextual

Session Learning Outcomes

At the end of the session, students will be able to

- analyze and create arguments in order to inform and persuade
- construct effective informative and persuasive messages (arguments) in order to display an accountable commitment to ethical practices[2]

Estimated Total Time Required

- In-class session: 60 minutes
- Individual sessions with students: approximately 45 minutes. Students can make more than one appointment with the librarian.
- Grading speech outline assessment activities: approximately 10 hours

Materials Needed

- Laptop for each group and access to internet
- Projector
- Whiteboard, markers
- Word documents with Proformas (Students are instructed to download these structured templates prior to the in-class session.)
- Information literacy tutorials
- Meeting space for individual consultations for students who take advantage of them

Learning Activities

1. Flipped instruction with information literacy tutorials. Given that there was time for one in-class library session, we decided to try a blended flipped classroom model. Students watched tutorials before the in-class session. The tutorial schedule was as follows:
   - Week 4: Learning and Information Veracity Tutorial (LIV@RIT) 1—Identifying Sources[3]
   - Week 5: LIV@RIT Tutorial 2—Choosing Topics; LIV@RIT Tutorial 4—Finding Articles; LIV@RIT Tutorial 5—Using the Web
   - Week 7: LIV@RIT Tutorial 7—Plagiarism and Copyright; LIV@RIT Tutorial 8—Citing Sources
2. Week 6: In-class instruction. Based on student reporting and tutorial quiz results, the librarian reinforced those concepts that were unclear.
   - Information search and evaluation
     - Model how to search the discovery tool for an e-book and an article.
     - Demonstrate how to refine a search.
     - Discuss how to decide if a certain book or article will have the material that fits the research need.
   - Course portfolio information literacy activity for the informative speech
     - Divide students into groups. Have group complete one informative speech Proforma (appendix LP7A).
     - Consult with each group during the process. Have students submit speech Proformas for feedback from the librarian.

Assessment

- Tutorial quizzes
  - Have students submit all quizzes because these quizzes are a mandatory assessment activity. Quizzes can be done as many times as needed before submitting a final version.

- Do not grade the quizzes. Review them to assess student understanding and retention of the concepts covered by each tutorial.
- In case any of the questions showed evidence of low understanding to no understanding, review these questions again in class.

- Informative speech Proforma, grading rubric (appendix LP7B)
  After the in-class session, students had until the following class to submit their speech Proforma. This assignment was a mandatory requirement in the process of creating the informative speech. This assignment counted for 5 percent of the total grade for the informative speech.
- Persuasive speech outline with Proforma, grading rubric
  In order to assess what was learned, we asked students to prepare a more detailed Proforma for the new assignment. In addition, a librarian-designed assessment included looking at an outline and commenting on the thesis statement and other information literacy elements already defined in the rubric for the persuasive speech Proforma. This assignment counted for 5 percent of the grade for the persuasive speech.
- Reflective essay[4] and reflective diary
  Drawing on the experience from a previous co-designing project done for a history course, students were asked to keep a reflective diary on a weekly basis. Diaries would reflect not only on the information literacy activities, but also on the overall course. These entries, together with the reflective essay that each student had to write at the end of the semester, were valuable sources of students' self-assessment on their learning progress throughout the course. Only through these contemplations were we able to truly have insight into metacognition and students' awareness and understanding of their own thought and learning processes. Only through the demonstration of the presence of certain cognitive and metacognitive abilities could we conclude whether metaliteracy is taking place, especially as it relates to the students' level of critical thinking.

APPENDIX LP7A

Proforma for the Informative and Public Speech

This Proforma is used for public speech.[5] The Proforma for the informative speech included only search strategy reporting and evaluation for journal article as a source.

Course:

Name and surname:

Search Strategy

Research Topic

1. Write down the topic that you will be researching (you can state this as a question or as a phrase).

Keywords

2. Split your phrase or question (from 1 above) into the key concepts. For example, if you were searching for *respiratory diseases among teenagers*, the key concepts (or keywords) are *respiratory tract diseases* and *teenagers.*

   In the top row of the table below, write each of your keywords. Then below each keyword, make a list of alternative keywords or phrases (meaning when more than one word creates the meaningful word cluster) that describe that concept. Think also about plurals, alternative spellings (e.g., color and colour), etc.

Example 1:

Concept 1	Concept 2	Concept 3
respiratory tract	diseases	teenagers
air pollution	health effects	adolescent
drug abuse	respiratory effects	
nicotine		

Example 2:

Concept 1	Concept 2	Concept 3
fear	crime	elderly
anxiety	victim	aged
phobia	mugging	pensioner
	robbery	oap

Concept Chart for Your Research

Note: you may not need all the columns or rows—it's okay to leave some blank or add more if required.

Concept 1	Concept 2	Concept 3

3. Write down the details of three searches you intend to use. Include one example of a broad search; the other examples should be narrower searches. You will also need to provide details of the Boolean operators that you will use to connect your keyword.

See the examples below:

Example 1:

Search 1	**respiratory tract AND diseases AND teenagers**	
Search 2	**air pollution** **AND health effects AND teenagers**	
Search 3	**respiratory effects** **AND drug abuse NOT nicotine**	

Example 2:

Search 1	**fear AND crime AND elderly**	
Search 2	**fear AND mugging AND elderly**	
Search 3		

Search 1		
Search 2		
Search 3		

Limits to the Search

4. Do you want to limit your search in any way? Examples of limits would be date, language, location, specific person(s) relevant to the topic, event(s) relevant to the topic, etc.

   Example 1: For my research for *respiratory diseases among teenagers*, I would ideally like information about the post-war Kosovo (since 2000).

   Example 2: For my research for *fear of crime among elderly people*, I would ideally like information about the UK from the last ten years.

Other Useful Notes

5. Do you already know the names of authors or organizations that might have published information on your topic? If you do, note these down below.

Where searched? **Database or search engine**	**Keyword combination**	**Any limits/ refining?**	**How many results?**	**Notes/comments**
Example: Google Scholar	air pollution AND teen-agers AND Kosovo	2000–2016, scholarly only	7,130	Results are to some extent relevant; however, many are about other countries. Could be helpful for comparing statistics with Kosovo.
Example: Google Scholar	air pollution AND Kosovo AND teenagers	2000–2016, scholarly only	6,890	Changing the place and putting Kosovo before teenagers, my search results became more relevant. There are still a lot of results looking at other countries, but I have three about Kosovo in the first few listed results.

Where searched? **Database or search engine**	**Keyword combination**	**Any limits/ refining?**	**How many results?**	**Notes/comments**
Example: RIT library search engine	air pollution AND health effects AND Kosovo AND adolescent	• full text online • scholarly & peer-reviewed • public health and medicine	39	Not very relevant. It is not a good strategy to use "health effects" as a keyword. It will not generate too relevant results. Some of the results could be used for general information about air pollution or adolescent health. However, nothing to look closely to my topic.
Example: RIT library search engine	air pollution AND respiratory effects AND Kosovo	• full text online • journal article • public health, medicine, sciences	72	Highly relevant results that mostly point directly to resources I'll be able to examine and use in my presentation.

Finding Journal and Journal Articles—Summary Sheet

Journal Article—Included

Search which retrieved this item (write down the number of the search attempt from the summary sheet):
Details of journal article citations in APA:

Permalink:

Write a one-paragraph description of the journal article. How useful was it for providing information on your topic? What will be particularly relevant?

Journal Article—Rejected

Search which retrieved this item (write down the number of the search attempt from the summary sheet):
Details of journal article citations in APA:

Permalink:

Write a one-paragraph description of the journal article. Explain why you chose to reject it for your research assignment.

Where searched **(Library database or search engine) with specific name**	**Keyword combination**	**Any limits/ refining?**	**How many results?**	**Notes/Comments**
Example: Ebook Central ProQuest (in the RIT electronic library)	fear AND crime AND elderly	2007–2017 UK	20,775	Many search results having to do with fear and crime in general. Some of the first listed books could be relevant for the introduction and general context.

Example: RIT search engine	fear AND crime AND elderly		2,213	To a certain extent relevant resources showed up as the first few listed. However, remaining results are not fully connected to what I need.
Example: Google Books	fear AND mugging AND elderly	2007–2017	6,500	Highly relevant. In the first page, I found at least 3 potential sources. Some are chapters in the book.

Finding e-Books and Book Chapters—Summary Sheet

E-book Record—Included

Search which retrieved this item (write down the number of the search attempt from the summary sheet):
Details of e-book, citation in APA:

Permalink:

Write a one-paragraph description of the eBook. How useful was it for providing information on your topic? What will be particularly relevant?

E-book Record—Rejected

Search which retrieved this item (write down the number of the search attempt from the summary sheet):
Details of e-book, citation in APA:

Permalink:

Write a one-paragraph description of the ebook. Explain why you chose to reject it for your research project.

Web Page/Site—Included

Details of web page/site, citation in APA:
Permalink:

Write a one-paragraph description of the web page/site. How did you find this website? Was it already familiar to you? How useful was it for providing information on your topic? What will be particularly relevant?

APPENDIX LP7B

Grading Rubric for the Informative Speech Proforma

Criteria	**Fully Correct** **2 Points**	**Fully Correct** **1.5 Points**	**Semi Correct** **1 Point**	**Semi Correct** **0.5 Point**
Citation	Manually created with minor punctuation errors	Citation tool–generated with minor punctuation errors	Effort obvious	No effort (i.e., same cases written differently)
Keywords	Clear aspects and understanding (topic, specific nouns/phrases, connectors)	Clear aspects and understanding with minor omissions or errors (connectors missing, only one example, etc.)	Unclear aspects (keywords mostly too general, no connectors)	
Criteria	**Fully Relevant** **4–3 Points**	**Fully Relevant** **2.5–1.5 Points**	**Partially Relevant** **1–0.5 Point**	
Search Process and Explanations	Research effort obvious; keywords fully relevant; refining elements relevant as well as selected sources; search process explanation focused, informative, and detailed	Minor omissions. Research effort obvious; keywords unfocused and general, refining elements do not relate specifically to the topic, search process explanation unfocused and informative	Some research effort obvious, with bigger issues or missing substantial elements of search process	

Criteria	**Fully Relevant** **1 Point**	**Fully Relevant** **1–0.5 Point**	**Partially Relevant** **0.5 Point**	
Types of Sources & Veracity	Information source appropriate and sound	Information source appropriate and unsound	Information source inappropriate but sound	

APPENDIX LP7C

Reflective Essay

Write a reflective essay on your experience with research assignments you had throughout this course (LIV@RIT tutorials with quizzes, outlines, and Proformas for speeches).[6] The purpose of this assignment is for you to develop and demonstrate the ability to

- evaluate your learning and performance
- assess personal struggles and development

Use the objectives listed above as a basis for your reflection, and answer the following:

- List three ways in which you think you have grown or developed because of these assignments.
- Which two of the LIV@RIT tutorials would you share with other students who did not attend this course? Why?
- What problems did you encounter in these assignments? How did you solve them?
- Describe something major you have learned about yourself from these assignments.

Notes

1. Linda Ziberi, "Public Speaking," (syllabus, RIT Kosovo (A.U.K), Prishtina, Kosovo, 2018).
2. In this lesson, as opposed to a previous project (see the lesson plan "A Historical Experiment in Historic Time: A Collaborative Effort toward a Different Information Literacy Experience"), we did not name any of the skill level outcomes, which are inevitably connected to both of the "big" outcomes we wanted students to grasp.
3. Learning Information Veracity @ RIT (LIV@RIT) are self-paced interactive tutorials designed by RIT Libraries at Rochester Institute of Technology. The set of eight tutorials can be found at https://library.rit.edu/liv/.
4. See appendix LP7C for the reflective essay questions.
5. This Proforma is based upon a Proforma created by Valerie Sonley et al., "Information Literacy Assessment by Portfolio: A Case Study," *Reference Services Review* 35, no. 1 (2007): 41–70, https://doi.org/10.1108/00907320710729355. Their Proforma is based on the Empire State College research portfolio.

6. For forming questions in this reflective essay, the book by Linda Suskie, *Assessing Student Learning* (Newark, NJ: John Wiley and Sons, 2018) was particularly helpful.

Bibliography

Sonley, Valerie, Denise Turner, Sue Myer, and Yvonne Cotton. "Information Literacy Assessment by Portfolio: A Case Study." *Reference Services Review* 35, no. 1 (2007): 41–70. https://doi.org/10.1108/00907320710729355.

Suskie, Linda. *Assessing Student Learning: A Common Sense Guide*. Newark, NJ: John Wiley and Sons, 2018.

LESSON PLAN 8

What's behind That?

Facts and Statistics Supporting Public Service Announcements

Livia Piotto

Reference and Instruction Coordinator, Frohring Library John Cabot University, Rome, Italy

Brief Course Description

Writing across the Media (COM 221) is a core required course for all students majoring in communications at John Cabot University. It is a writing-intensive course that exposes students to different writing techniques for a variety of formats used in the media professions and in digital multimedia production. The course aims to prepare the students for careers in the media while, at the same time, they gain practical skills that combine researching and writing.

The course is structured into four different modules, each of which builds up to an individual assignment that exposes the students to a specific writing mode.[1] Each module, and consequently each assignment, offered the possibility of integrating information literacy components that would have addressed specific research skills the students could incorporate in their writing projects.

Student Level

The course is intended for freshmen and sophomores majoring in communications. Given that John Cabot University has a varied student body that includes both resident degree-seeking students and study-abroad students (mostly from the US), there might be older students from different disciplines attending the course, but for the most part this is a course with a predominance of freshman and sophomore degree-seeking students.

Context for the Lesson

This lesson plan was developed for the second module of COM 221, which culminates in a public service announcement (PSA) script as the final assignment. The students have to write the script and storyboard for a PSA about a organization related to the topic chosen for the blog they curated in the first module of the course.

This librarian-facilitated session takes place after an introductory class on public service announcements. No preliminary work is required prior to the session, but the students already have gained some basic research skills in a prior library session.

Frames Addressed

- Information Creation as a Process
- Searching as Strategic Exploration

Session Learning Outcomes

At the end of the session students will be able to

- categorize evidence types (e.g., facts, statistics, statements, and opinions) in order to identify source types that are likely to contain that information
- apply appropriate search strategies in order to collect information from various source types that will help them create a persuasive message for a PSA

Estimated Total Time Required

75 minutes

Materials Needed

- Computers or tablets with internet access for student use. At JCU we have a "mobile lab" equipped with tablets, but we often rely on a BYOD practice,

which is fairly easy to do, especially with communications students who are used to working on their own devices.
- Instructor computer and projector
- Whiteboard and markers
- Type of Content fact sheet (see appendix LP8A)

Learning Activities

1. Introduction to the session
   The session begins with the librarian describing the learning outcomes and providing an overview of the online course guide.[2]

2. Write-Pair-Share
   In the first segment of the session, the librarian asks the students to write possible types of evidence that they might need to support the message in their PSA (e.g., facts, statistics, statements, and opinions). The students are then paired up to discuss their lists with a partner. The discussion aims to give to the students the possibility of having their work reviewed by a peer who might have helpful suggestions. Then students share out with the larger group while the librarian takes note of the group suggestions on the whiteboard.
   With this initial activity the students are asked to assess how the creation of a PSA fits their information needs in terms of type of evidence that they might need.[3]

3. Analysis of types of evidence
   After collecting suggestions about different types of evidence that might be used in a PSA, the librarian engages the students in a conversation about where various types of evidence and information might be published and how they are disseminated to a larger audience (scholarly research, news articles, blogs, consumer reports, etc.).
   The group discusses which publication types might include the evidence the students have identified as relevant for supporting their PSA message. The discussion serves to highlight the relationships between evidence types and publication types. It allows students to focus and

reflect on the type of publications they need to search in order to answer their questions, and it connects back with the frame Searching as Strategic Exploration because it gives the students the opportunity to think how they can access information based on who produces it.

4. Type of content activity and independent research time
   Before beginning the type of content activity, the librarian briefly introduces some core resources (the library's discovery tool, databases with scholarly publications, statistics reports, etc.) and demonstrates how to access different types of publications.
   Then the librarian distributes the Type of Content fact sheet (appendix LP8A), which asks students to document the type of evidence they need to support the message in their PSA. The librarian explains how to conduct research for the PSA and how to fill in the fact sheet. The worksheet can also be an online document that the students have to fill in, giving them the opportunity to access their research even after the session is over. Because this is a practice activity followed by a homework assignment, there is no need for the librarian to return the fact sheets to the students.
   Following the prompt, the students start exploring library and web resources to collect sources that include supporting evidence for their PSA.
   The librarian and the professor rove around the class to help students and answer individual questions.
   While conducting their research, the students fill in the fact sheet with examples of facts and statistics, opinions, and quotations that could support their main PSA claim.
   During this activity the students understand how to develop a complex search strategy and to adapt it for creating a specific artifact, combining the two frames addressed by the lesson plan.

5. Closing and wrap-up
   At the end of the session the librarian collects the fact sheets for the observational assessment and invites the students to reflect and report on problems and issues they have encountered and on searching strategies they have found particularly useful and they want to share with

the rest of the group. The library session and its activity are preparatory for a homework assignment during which the students have to replicate the strategies used during the in-class activity.

Assessment

In-class formative assessment happens during the Write-Pair-Share activity,[4] which provides a snapshot of what the students think might be a solid source they could use to support their main claim and create a persuasive message in their PSA. The following discussion provides a measure of students' understanding of basic research skills and different source types they can encounter during the research process.

As in the lesson plan "Evaluating News through the Exploration of Bias," observational assessment was used to assess level 2 (Learning) of the Kirkpatrick Model.[5] The Type of Content fact sheet was paired with a success matrix (table LP8.1) aimed at assessing if and how the students have engaged with the activity.[6] The success matrix was accompanied by the librarian's reflective comments about the unfolding of the activity and the students' reception of the information covered during the session.

Table LP8.1

Evaluating controversial news activity success matrix

Indicator	Level 3: Success	Level 2: Partial Success	Level 1: Little Success
Students completed the fact sheet in all its parts	More than 75% of attendees	50–75% of attendees	Less than 50% of attendees
Students categorized the different evidence types	More than 75% of worksheets	50–75% of worksheets	Less than 50% of worksheets
Students retrieved appropriate source types matching the evidence needed	More than 75% of worksheets	50–75% of worksheets	Less than 50% of worksheets

APPENDIX LP8A

Type of Content Fact Sheet

What type of evidence do you need to support the message in your PSA?

Type of content	**Your content and sources used**
Facts and statistics Facts and statistics will support your claims and will make up the majority of good persuasive PSAs. Remember to record accurately all facts and statistics from your sources. You will not necessarily need a list of your sources in the PSA, but all the claims made must be verifiable.	
Opinions All PSAs are planned to be persuasive. To do so you can share your opinions, possibly based on verifiable facts (see above), but you also have to include other people's opinions. In any case, opinions need to be backed up somehow. Be sure to use words and phrases that convey the emotion that you're hoping to communicate!	
Quotations Do not underestimate the power of a good quotation! Quotations from recognized experts or the people closest to your issue can be particularly persuasive and convey the message better than anything else. You can also use quotations from people in show business: they can become the champions for your PSA!	

Notes

1. See also the case study titled "Integrating Information Literacy in a Communication Writing Course" and the first library session's lesson plan titled "Evaluating News through the Exploration of Bias."
2. The course guide is a sub-page of the general Communications LibGuide developed for the major. The guide is available at https://johncabot.libguides.com/communications/COM221, and it includes resources and activities used in the library sessions.
3. See the knowledge practice "assess the fit between an information product's creation process and a particular information need" under the frame Information Creation as a Process in Association of College and Research Libraries, *Framework for Information Literacy for Higher Education* (Chicago: Association of College and Research Libraries, 2016), http://www.ala.org/acrl/standards/ilframework.
4. Melissa Bowles-Terry and Cassandra Kvenild, *Classroom Assessment Techniques for Librarians* (Chicago: Association of College and Research Libraries, 2015), 33.
5. Donald L. Kirkpatrick and James D. Kirkpatrick, *Evaluating Training Programs*, 3rd ed. (San Francisco: Berrett-Koehler, 2006).
6. The success matrix was developed using an example included in Candice Benjes-Small et al., "Teaching Web Evaluation: A Cognitive Development Approach," *Communications in Information Literacy* 7, no. 1 (2013): 39, https://doi.org/10.15760/comminfolit.2013.7.1.133.

Bibliography

Association of College and Research Libraries. *Framework for Information Literacy for Higher Education*. Chicago: Association of College and Research Libraries, 2016. http://www.ala.org/acrl/standards/ilframework.

Benjes-Small, Candice, Alyssa Archer, Katelyn Tucker, Lisa Vassady, and Jennifer Resor Whicker. "Teaching Web Evaluation: A Cognitive Development Approach." *Communications in Information Literacy* 7, no. 1 (2013): 39–49. https://doi.org/10.15760/comminfolit.2013.7.1.133.

Bowles-Terry, Melissa, and Cassandra Kvenild. *Classroom Assessment Techniques for Librarians*. Chicago: Association of College and Research Libraries, 2015.

Kirkpatrick, Donald L., and James D. Kirkpatrick. *Evaluating Training Programs: The Four Levels*, 3rd ed. San Francisco: Berrett-Koehler, 2006.

LESSON PLAN 9

Research in the Discipline

Fatmeh Charafeddine

Associate University Librarian, Research and Academic Collaboration Services, University Libraries, American University of Beirut, Lebanon

Brief Course Description

English 300, Writing in the Disciplines, is a course designed to assist students with their graduate-level writing in English. The course begins with an introduction to academic writing in general and then moves to doing research and writing in specific disciplines. Students are requested to work in groups of three to five students to design and conduct research in their academic field. Part of the course focuses on introducing information literacy skills including locating relevant resources, learning advanced search techniques and strategies, evaluating information, understanding copyright issues, and considering the ways scholars work collaboratively and deal with issues of intellectual property and plagiarism.

Student Level

Students taking English 300 course are usually in their first semester as graduate students at the American University of Beirut (AUB). Many of them are international students from other Arab countries or come from other universities in Lebanon. They have very different backgrounds in information literacy, writing skills, and doing research. Students in this class need to learn about the different types of information, where and how to find relevant information, and how to assess, select, and use information in an effective and responsible way. The number of students taking the class is twenty.

Context for the Lesson

Students in the English 300 class come from different academic majors. It is very important for them to understand how knowledge is created and disseminated in their different fields of research.

This is the second library session out of four sessions that are integrated in the course.

The first session covers the importance of understanding the different mediums and types of information and how each type is assessed and used.[1]

This second session, focuses on information retrieval and use in a specific subject area. Before starting their research, students need to explore different information resources in their research area, identify the key issues surrounding their research topic, and become familiar with the writings of the prominent scholars in the field. Learning how to do a literature review will introduce them to the scholarly conversation surrounding their topic with its different branches and perceptions. Exploring the conversation will help them think about how they can contribute to it by adding new findings, using new perspectives, challenging an existing conclusion, or asking new questions. While contributing to the conversation, it is important that researchers provide their sources of information and recognize the contributions of other authors.

Frames Addressed

- **Scholarship as Conversation:** Looking at scholarly works, students will notice that research in any field is an open conversation based on previous findings and is always developing and branching out.
- **Authority Is Constructed and Contextual:** Because knowledge is cumulative, authors need to give credit to each other by citing the sources of their information.
- **Searching as Strategic Exploration:** With the availability of and easy access to online information, students need to learn how to search for information effectively and how to make the best use of library resources.

Session Learning Outcomes

- Locate specialized resources using the library subject databases and journal lists.
- Find articles with literature reviews and start your own literature review.
- Find resources according to certain criteria such as peer-reviewed, date range, author, or source title.
- Use information responsibly by giving credit to consulted sources.

Estimated Total Time Required

90 minutes

Venue

Classroom in the English department

Materials Needed

- Laptop, projector, and screen for the PowerPoint presentation
- Assignment from the previous session (more information in the Learning Activities section)
- Hands-on venue: The Antoun Ghattas Karam E-classroom is equipped with advanced technology aiming at providing an interactive class environment for instruction and workshop sessions. The e-classroom can accommodate up to thirty students and has thirty all-in-one desktop computers with twenty-three-inch touch screens and a podium with a nineteen-inch HD touch screen.
- Consulted tools: Sage Research Methods Database, including the modules on
  - key concepts in research
  - philosophy of research
  - research ethics
  - research design
  - research project planner

Learning Activities

1. **Report and discuss the assignment from the previous session (30 minutes).**

   - Ask a selection of students to briefly present to the class their findings for one of the questions of the assignment from the previous session:

     - Use the library webpage to locate different types of resources for your research topic (e.g., books, news, scholarly articles). Bring a list of your findings to the next class.
     - Find one article in Wikipedia about your topic.
     - Explain briefly how you are going to use each source to support your research paper.
     - Find and scan the bibliography in one or more of the located resources and demonstrate how research is usually documented.

   - Discuss student answers with the class. The instructor and the librarian take notes to include in the final course assessment report.
   - The class instructor collects the assignment from students to assess learning outcomes for session 1.

2. **PowerPoint presentation with online access to the library resources (30 minutes)**
   In this presentation students are instructed on how to find information in their field of research, how to use reference sources to find background information, what the subject databases in their field are, and how to search the library catalog by subject.
   Does research provide final answers, or is it ongoing conversation? Students reflect on the question and start a short discussion. The role of the literature review is then described as the perfect introduction to main issues surrounding the scholarly conversation, the authors contributing to the conversation, and the cumulative knowledge about a specific topic. Students are encouraged to do their own literature review, which will help them work on their research question

by defining the context of their research, selecting their research method, and identifying the type of needed materials (primary and secondary, reference, popular or peer-reviewed, textual or audiovisual). Using one of the multidisciplinary databases, the librarian then demonstrates how to search for special types of materials and how to use search limits and results filters to find resources in specific date ranges, by specific authors, or from specific publications. Recognizing that research is a collaborative work with unlimited potential to branch out and add new perspectives, students are alerted to the importance of giving credit to previous research by always keeping records of their sources and properly citing them.

3. **Class activities, hands-on exercise (30 minutes)**

   - Students are divided into groups of three to five students working on the Sage research project for the class. Students are assigned to work collaboratively to choose the terms to use in searching for resources for their group term papers for the class.
   - All students in all groups work on their own, using the workstations in the e-classroom to search the subject databases and the library catalog. Students are asked to find a recent book or thesis about their topic and an article with a literature review for the topic of their group paper.
   - The faculty member and the librarian move around listening to the conversation and trying to help as needed.
   - Students come together as a class again. A student from each group reports briefly on the literature review found by the group members.

Assessment: Take-Home Quiz

Assessment happens as observation by the librarian and instructor during the class activities and through the take-home quiz, which is discussed in the next session as a learning activity and handed in to the class instructor for assessment.

1. Search a specialized encyclopedia to find an article on the subject of your group paper.

2. Search the databases in your subject area and find a recent (after 2017) peer-reviewed article covering your research topic.
3. Find an article on your topic with a good literature review section.
4. When searching a database, export the citations of your selected articles from your results list according to your selected citation style.
5. Name a peer-reviewed journal published by a scientific society in your field of research.

The quiz is collected first thing in the next library instruction session to English 300 class.

APPENDIX LP9A

Consulted Books

Blanchett, Helen, Chris Powis, and Jo Webb. *A Guide to Teaching Information Literacy: 101 Practical Tips*. London: Facet, 2012.

Bravender, Patricia, Hazel McClure, and Gayle Schaub, eds. *Teaching Information Literacy Threshold Concepts: Lesson Plans for Librarians.* Chicago: Association of College and Research Libraries, 2015.

Burkhardt, Joanna M, and Mary C. MacDonald with Andrée J. Rathemacher. *Teaching Information Literacy: 50 Standards-Based Exercises for College Students.* Chicago: American Library Association, 2010.

Note

1. See also the lesson plan of session one, titled "Getting Started with Graduate Research."

LESSON PLAN 10

A Historical Experiment in Historic Time

A Collaborative Effort toward a Different Information Literacy Experience

Ivana Stevanović

Institutional Librarian, RIT Kosovo (A.U.K), Kosovo

This lesson plan describes an initiative started in fall 2015, when Professor Erik Benson and I experimented with trying to trace and successfully trigger metaliteracy with freshman level students in his Twentieth Century Europe history course (HIST170). We experimented with integrating the frames from the 2015 draft proposal of the ACRL *Framework for Information Literacy for Higher Education* at different points for assignments and assessments in HIST170.[1] In this project, we collaborated to create and assess course assignments that included an information literacy component.

In Dr. Benson, I found an eager supporter and advocate for information literacy. Dr. Benson appreciated my view of information literacy, which has always looked beyond student skill acquisition and more toward metaliteracy. When we first spoke, he expected me to help students with citations and introduce library subscription databases. After our initial conversation, we decided to embark on a much more ambitious project: to look into deeply individual occurrence, which meant we tracked evidence of cognitive abilities being triggered and applied in an assignment.

We designed a group information literacy session organized outside of class time with Dr. Benson and me; students were also encouraged to attend individual meetings with the librarian. Dr. Benson made the group session with the librarian mandatory, and he also planned to attend the session. With these information literacy sessions, we aimed to make sure students were given an opportunity to learn information and research basics, and we hoped to spark student curiosity for knowledge.

The whole information literacy experience has been given weight because credit was given. Students received extra credit equivalent to 10 percent of the course project grade if they attended the information literacy group session; if they did not attend, they would have the same amount deducted from their final assignment grade. In addition, students had other information literacy–specific assignments worth approximately 15 percent of their final course grade.

Brief Course Description

As described in the course syllabus: "Twentieth Century Europe (HIST170), examines major themes and controversies in European history from 1900 to the present, placing an emphasis on the early twentieth-century crisis of liberal democracy and the political alternatives proposed to parliamentary government: right-wing nationalism, communism, and fascism. Special attention will be placed on racial politics and immigration, state surveillance regimes, and European debates over Americanization and globalization of European cultures."[2]

Student Level

This course is intended mostly for freshmen.

Context for the Lesson

The group information literacy session was held outside of class time. Students were given time slots to sign up to attend a group information literacy session.

All sessions took place two weeks before an outline for the annotated bibliography assignment was due. In the syllabus students were required to meet with the librarian prior to submitting their project outline. Students also were asked to identify minimally a general topic for their final research assignment. We thought the group information literacy session and the requirement to meet with the librarian would prolong student exposure to information literacy and get freshmen into the habit of using reference services.

Frames Addressed

- Searching as Strategic Exploration
- Research as Inquiry
- Information Creation as a Process

Session Learning Outcomes

At the end of this session students will be able to

- distinguish between different item types and the ways various items are used in research
- successfully narrow down a topic
- search for relevant resources for their research
- apply knowledge, the mental path," when selecting resources they find independently as evidence of metacognition[3]

Estimated Total Time Required

- Each group information literacy session lasted approximately 75 minutes, with three time slots available for students to attend.
- Individual sessions with students lasted approximately 45 minutes.

Materials Needed

- Laptops (or desktop computers)
- Internet access
- Projector

- Whiteboard, markers
- Existing online quiz game
- Paper slips with Muddiest Point questions

Learning Activities

Students were to work individually on their laptops on each learning activity using their topic. The only class-wide activity was an online quiz game that is part of the Learning Information Veracity tutorials.[4] The online quiz game is played after the tutorial "Identifying Sources." In addition, for each activity, I had an example on the whiteboard or projected on the screen that we would go through as a group before students complete each activity for their individual topics on laptops.

1. Frame addressed in this section: Research as Inquiry

   - Choose and narrow topic:

     - Review the syllabus and assignment requirements. In our local context, culture is more oral rather than written, and I noticed that reminding students of the location of assignment details in the syllabus is essential for their proper understanding of what is expected from them.
     - Brainstorm and narrow topics. The general topics that students had already prepared are further narrowed based on specifics related to each topic. For students who did not select a general topic, we asked those individuals to start from their interests to decide on a topic. We introduced the Credo Reference database as a reference source that can be a starting point for thinking about interests; introducing this database also provides the librarian with the opportunity to explain what databases are in general. Lastly, after students have decided on their topics, they work together to narrow their topics to help formulate a thesis or research question.

   - Group exercise: Formulate keywords for searching, using a student topic as an example.

2. Frame addressed in this section: Searching as Strategic Exploration
   - Review types of resources:
     - Students identify different types of sources: books, e-books, journals, magazines, and reference materials.
     - The librarian explains different types of sources and compares sources in detail.
     - The librarian leads a discussion about how to use different sources in academic essays and research papers.
     - Group exercise and a game: Students are tasked with locating the best source for their project. They complete the online quiz game "LIV@RIT Meter" at http://library.rit.edu/liv/1-6.
   - Search for and evaluate information:
     - The librarian describes the discovery tool (Summon) as a general information search tool. The librarian demonstrates how to structure a search:
       - how to search for an e-book and articles
       - how to refine a search in Summon
       - how to use subject description previews, abstracts, or summaries to locate an article
     - Librarian demonstrates how to use Boolean connectors.
     - Students then practice how to determine if a book or article will suit their research needs both in groups and individually.
     - Students participate in guided practice with searching for e-books. The librarian and the professor provide additional instruction about the value of e-books for research purposes and guidance on how to selectively read an e-book. I have noticed that our entry-level students fear using books or e-books as resources, thinking that they are obliged always to read the whole book from cover to cover if they select it as a resource. Dr. Benson and I jointly reassured students that they are not bad academics if they opt for selective reading in certain cases.

- If time allows, the librarian explains in detail how to access an article and how to acquire articles not available immediately online.

Integrated Assessment

- Information literacy group session assignments
- Identification of sources
- In-class group quiz game "LIV@RIT Meter" covering selecting the most fitting types of sources for the assignment[5]
- Muddiest Point classroom assessment technique
- Final paper assessment

The outline assignment was due after students learned how to create outlines and how to annotate bibliographies in an English course. Both Dr. Benson and I graded the outline assignment. Fifty percent of the final grade for the outline was allocated for information literacy assessment. As the librarian I was responsible for reviewing sources, citation in Chicago Turabian style, annotated bibliography, and research question.

Reflective Questionnaire

We used a questionnaire based on the article "The One-Minute Paper and the One-Hour Class: Outcomes Assessment for One-Shot Library Instruction,"[6] recommended to us by Susan Mee, global, online and university studies librarian at Rochester Institute of Technology in New York.

The reflective questionnaire for HIST 170 Twentieth Century Europe included the following questions:

1. How did you decide on the thesis/research question? (Briefly explain the process/steps which led to this decision.)
2. What will determine how narrowed your research topic should be?
3. How can you tell if an article is from a scholarly source or from a popular magazine?

4. How can you ensure more relevant results when searching for materials?
5. Why did you choose the specific sources as your reference? (Explain briefly how were these, according to you, better fitting for your assignment than some others you encountered.)

Adding this questionnaire was an ad hoc idea where students were to answer questions and submit them with their final papers. We wanted to triangulate the data for analysis of the success of the whole project. In addition, we realized that the outline as we made it did not provide enough data for each student to help us explore the metacognitive creation process. We thought the reflective questions might strengthen our claim that students had applied cognitive abilities to their research assignment.

Research Paper

In order to determine if our one-semester experiment, consisting of an information literacy group session, guided librarian-faculty mentoring, and a few points of information literacy assessment, will show the presence of metaliteracy, we wanted to create a faculty-librarian rubric to assess a sample of the students' final papers. This activity remained unfinished because we left the final making of the rubric for after the semester started. It proved impossible to do this once the classes resumed.

Notes

1. Association of College and Research Libraries, *Framework for Information Literacy for Higher Education* (Chicago: Association of College and Research Libraries, 2016).
2. Benson, Erik, "20th Century Europe," (syllabus, RIT Kosovo (A.U.K), Prishtina, Kosovo, 2015).
3. The last outcome is something impossible to reach in the one-shot session. Students need a good command of cognitive abilities to think, learn, remember, connect, reason, analyze, and synthesize. These processes take time and repetition in different situations; however, we wanted to try to track evidence of these abilities being triggered and applied to an assignment. The follow-up, as we planned it, through individual mentoring and additional

points of assessment and guiding, was necessary to confirm whether metacognition is taking place.

4. Learning Information Veracity (LIV@RIT) are self-paced interactive tutorials designed by RIT Libraries at Rochester Institute of Technology. This set of eight tutorials can be found at https://library.rit.edu/liv/.
5 Link to the online quiz: http://library.rit.edu/liv/1-6.
6. Elizabeth Choinski and Michelle Emanuel, "The One-Minute Paper and the One-Hour Class: Outcomes Assessment for One-Shot Library Instruction," *Reference Services Review* 34, no. 1 (2006): 148–55, https://doi.org/10.1108/00907320610648824.

Bibliography

Association of College and Research Libraries. *Framework for Information Literacy for Higher Education*. Chicago: Association of College and Research Libraries, 2016.

Choinski, Elizabeth, and Michelle Emanuel. "The One-Minute Paper and the One-Hour Class: Outcomes Assessment for One-Shot Library Instruction." *Reference Services Review* 34, no. 1 (2006): 148–55. https://doi.org/10.1108/00907320610648824.

About the Authors

Fatmeh Charafeddine, is associate university librarian, Research and Academic Collaboration Services, at the University Libraries, American University of Beirut. She has an MLS degree from Simmons College and a master's degree in Middle Eastern studies from the University of Toronto. She focuses on developing specialized library instruction and research services. And she is active in building collaborative initiatives across and beyond the university campus to create information retrieval solutions for underdiscovered collections and resources.

Aziz El Hassani is a research and learning services supervisor at Al Akhawayn University in Ifrane Library. He holds a master's degree from the University of Malta, a bachelor's degree in English language and literature, and recently completed the Library Leadership in the Digital Age program at the Harvard Graduate School of Education, Harvard University. Address correspondence to Aziz El Hassani, Al Akhawayn University, Mohammed VI Library, Ifrane, 53000, Morocco (e-mail: a.elhassani@aui.ma).

Najla Jarkas is a senior lecturer in the English department at the American University of Beirut. She received her MA and PhD from the University of Reading, UK. She is the chair of the Digital Scholarship Committee and member coordinator for the Digital Humanities at AMICAL Consortium. She currently serves on the coordinating committee of the Digital Humanities Institute—Beirut 2019. Her recent research interests are in the field of digital humanities. She is currently working on a digital humanities project on the Orientalists.

Christine Furno earned her master of library science and master of information science degrees from Indiana University Bloomington. She has been working at the American University of Sharjah since 2002. Currently working as the reference and instruction librarian, she has professional interests that include reflective teaching practices, IL assessment, and library marketing initiatives.

Samantha Godbey is education librarian and associate professor at the University of Nevada, Las Vegas. She earned her MLIS from San José State University and an MA in education from the University of California at Berkeley. Samantha is a presenter with the ACRL Roadshow "Engaging with the ACRL Framework: A Catalyst for Exploring and Expanding Our Teaching Practices" and is coeditor of *Disciplinary Applications of Information Literacy Threshold Concepts* (ACRL, 2017). Her research focuses on information literacy instruction and assessment.

Xan Goodman is a health sciences librarian and associate professor at the University of Nevada, Las Vegas, where she supports three schools in the Division of Health Sciences: the School of Integrated Health Sciences, the School of Public Health, and the School of Nursing. She has presented extensively at national and international conferences about information literacy, health sciences librarianship, and threshold concepts. She earned her master's degree in library and information science (MLIS) from Wayne State University.

Stavros Hadjisolomou is an assistant professor of psychology at the American University of Kuwait. He holds degrees in psychology (BA, MPhil, and PhD) from the City University of New York. In his research experience, he conducted interdisciplinary studies on cognition, brain, and behavior in both humans and animals from the perspectives of behavioral neuroscience, psychology, and biology. He is currently conducting research exploring causal factors underlying learning in students of all ages and the influence of technology on cognition, learning, and wellness.

Antonio Lopez, PhD, is a leading international specialist in media literacy education. He has written four books: *Mediacology: A Multicultural Approach to Media Literacy in the 21st Century* (Peter Lang, 2008), *The Media Ecosystem: What Ecology Can Teach Us about Responsible Media Practice* (Evolver Editions, 2012), *Greening Media Education* (Peter Lang, 2014), and *Ecomedia Literacy: Integrating Ecology into Media Education* (Routledge, 2020). He has published numerous journal articles and book chapters about media education, youth media, and ecomedia literacy. He is currently associate professor and chair of communications and media studies at John Cabot University in Rome, Italy.

Paul M. Love, Jr. received his PhD in Near Eastern studies from the University of Michigan. He is currently assistant professor of North Africa, Middle Eastern, and Islamic studies at Al Akhawayn University in Ifrane, Morocco, where he teaches courses in history and Islamic studies. His research focuses on premodern Islamic history in the Maghrib, the Arabic manuscript tradition, and Ibadi Muslim communities.

Elizabeth Macias-Gutiérrez is a lecturer in the Communications Department at John Cabot University. She holds a PhD in documentary theatre and multimedia performance from the Center for Contemporary and Digital Performance at Brunel University London (UK), an MA in intercultural communication from the University of Sheffield (UK), and a BSc in journalism from Abilene Christian University in Texas (USA). She has taught a variety of courses at John Cabot University, the Tecnológico de Monterrey in México (Campus Laguna), and the American University of Rome (AUR). Courses taught include Writing across the Media, Journalism in Theory and Practice, Commercial and Corporate Video Design, Cultural Theory, Public Speaking, Composition, and Writing for Business.

Livia Piotto started working at John Cabot University as reference librarian in 2006, and she is now reference and instruction coordinator. She earned her master's degree in library science from University of Rome "La Sapienza." In her role at John Cabot University, she coordinates reference and instruction services, and she is the liaison for business and social sciences. She is currently serving on the AMICAL Information Literacy Committee.

Meaghan Scott Seyve intertwines entrepreneurship into every class she teaches. She was a lecturer in marketing in a global environment and entrepreneurship at the American University of Paris from 2014 to 2018, as well as teaching master's level courses in marketing and multicultural management at Le Cnam. Mixing creative ideas and business development with information science and data research rooted her classes in practical hands-on experiences for students. She is an international business development consultant and a seasoned entrepreneur. Meaghan holds an MBA from Babson with a semester exchange at HEC Paris and currently lives in Silicon Valley.

Jorge F. Sosa (Quito), formerly chief librarian at the Latin American Faculty of Social Sciences, Ecuador, and at Universidad San Francisco de Quito, has an MSLS (UK, with a Fulbright/LASPAU scholarship) and an MA in human resources (CNAM, Paris). He collaborated in the implementation of a special LIS program at Universidad Técnica Particular de Loja/Fulbright Commission of Ecuador. Since 2006, he has worked as university librarian at the American University of Paris and has never stopped teaching information literacy at his institution.

Krasimir Spasov is currently the information literacy and reference librarian at Panitza Library at the American University in Bulgaria (AUBG). He holds a library science master's degree from Sofia University, Bulgaria, and is a recent ACRL Immersion alumnus. In addition to teaching and planning, Krasimir is also involved in the coordination, marketing, and evaluation of the AUBG information literacy program. He serves as the faculty liaison for all general inquiries on library instruction at AUBG and is an active member of the AMICAL Information Literacy Committee.

Ivana Stevanović is institutional librarian at AUK/RIT Kosovo. With experience as a lecturer, journalist, student and human rights activist, and researcher in humanities, Ivana uses her diverse experience in an attempt to rethink the role of the library in the students' active learning and application of knowledge. She is an advocate for lifelong learning and responsible lifestyle. Her current focus includes information literacy, digital literacy, critical thinking, and design thinking. Ivana holds MAs in media and communication and in comparative and Serbian literature. She has been an AMICAL Information Literacy Committee member since 2017.

Michael Stöpel is the user services librarian for the American University of Paris. Originally from Munich (Germany), he joined the American University of Paris in 2001. He received his MA in library and information science (MLIS) in 2010 from the Information School at the Humbold University in Berlin, Germany. Before coming to AUP, Michael Stöpel studied sociology in Munich and in Paris. He is currently serving on the AMICAL Information Literacy Committee.

Tatev Zargaryan is currently working for the American University of Armenia as a library systems and e-services librarian. She holds a diploma in library and information services from the Robert Gordon University, Scotland. She is an information literacy librarian and also an ACRL Immersion 2018 alumna. She also acts as an e-learning instructional designer and at the same time manages the open access library system DSpace for AGBU Papazian Library. She has served on the AMICAL Information Literacy Committee since 2015.